THE HISTORY AND FUTURE OF SCIENCE
AND TECHNOLOGY IN AFRICA

THE LAST DIGITAL FRONTIER

ASINGIA

Dedication:

To my family; the world is yours and dreams

with action do come true!

A special **wasingia** (thank you) to Brandy Lellou without which this book and media project would still be just a dream; Brenda Lare for her editorial patience and contributions; Franco Abott and his family especially the wife Rachel Abott for the friendship, business partnership and mental support. Sincerely grateful to our Kiva campaign backers, business customers, alma mater alumni, educators, investors, students and the African youth all over the world who are the inspiration for this book.

"Dear reader, wasingia (thank you) for buying a copy of this book. The digital version is discounted if bought alongside the print purchase. A **podcast**, **report** and **web series** with the same title *The Last Digital Frontier* is available on all major platforms including **DreamGalaxy TV** for your voice or immersive multimedia reviews, feedback, questions and dreams. This book is a start of my one book per year commitment to compliment my TV series ***The One Who Lives Forever*** and feature film franchise ***Middle Ground***, please share the book with a friend, family member, book club, class or recommend it to your librarian for acquisition or invite me to speak as keynote, panelist or delve into the topics in here through a masterclass. With your financial and community support, we can not only educate, entertain but also build the next generation of Africapitalists. Join, support and share *The Last Digital Frontier* community at **www.brianasingia.com**

Table of Contents

The Last Digital Frontier

The History and Future of Science and

Technology in Africa.

Preface by Brandy Lellou, Director of Infrastructure - DreamAfrica Consulting

This book tells a long overdue and timeless story of the rise of mankind in Africa, uncovers inventions and innovations across the continent throughout time, and paints a forecast of its digital revolution in the 21st century and beyond. For too long the birthplaces of "the world's religions" have been revered with annual pilgrimages, holidays and stories that have stood the test of time. However, the birthplace of humankind has been forgotten; lost in the history books, souls, and celebrations of modern-day Homo Sapiens. Through interviews with prominent African figures and the most recent research and insights from archeologists, scientists, and historians, hear the long overdue and timeless tale, ***The Last Digital Frontier: The History and Future of Science and Technology in Africa*** as told by ASINGIA and other African voices.

The Last Digital Frontier is divided into four parts that take readers on a journey through Africa. From the dawn of mankind's internal awareness (IA) to the development of Artificial Intelligence (AI) and beyond, each part explores a wave of development, discovery, infrastructure, technology and science. The book provides a compelling historic and forward-looking exploration of "the last digital frontier" of access and inclusion, Africa, and its potential to lead, host, and create the innovation breakthroughs of the future.

Introduction

Part one gives a historical account of the advent of mankind in Africa and his/her experimental stages with fire, tools, and language, as well as the development of early agriculture, and the little known, infrastructure and civilizations that rose across the continent and then spread throughout the world.

Part two uncovers the early influence migration and trade had on Africa and the later theft of history, culture, technology and dignity under the auspice of 'enlightenment' as Africa's descendants returned as "white men".

Part three draws back the virtual curtain of the last fifty years and unveils the silent scientific, artistic and digital revolution that has been occurring on the continent.

Part four lays out Africa's early adoption culture and rapid practical innovation of technology and the way it is transforming the continent towards a promising future of transparent ownership, trust centered collaborations and value-based exchanges, backed by digitized identities and cultures.

Preface: Origins - From Internal Awareness (IA) to Artificial Intelligence (AI)

"And remember Son, you are the son of the soil!" my father would remind me with a wink and a nod or smile depending on the context of why I needed the reminder or words of encouragement. I do not recall when he first said it, but I remember it and associate it with my most important decision making moments; the morning of the National Exams in Uganda, the start of my journey to study abroad in the US, my first interview for a job at The New York Stock Exchange, my decision to start my first company and yes even writing this book. Even today, when he is miles away from me, I whisper these words to myself when the moment inspires me to and here they are in this book.

I have never asked him directly what he means by the expression, and a part of me knows it started with our childhood moments, perhaps an evolution of a joke or statement I made while we visited my grandparents. I am a son of the soil, a son of the land, the mountains of the moon (Mt. Rwenzori), the valleys and rivers that flow through it. I am my ancestors, their dreams, their wisdom, their blessings and stories. I am Africa. I am ASINGIA.

Growing up, in Kasese, Uganda, among the Bakonzo, speaking Lukonzo and often identifying with my neighbors across the river in DRC (the Democratic Republic of Congo), and only learning orally, as Lukonzo was then an unwritten language, curiosity was the key to answers, to knowledge, history and the world.

Folk stories, questions and answer conversations with family, relatives and elders was my early childhood education.

The discovery of books, libraries, school and now computers or electronics powered by the internet has made me appreciate the value of Africa's history, my history and story. This is my history of Africa. I believe everyone has a story, so in Chinua Achebe's words: "If you don't like someone's story, write your own." This is my own.

I first interacted with a computer in 2006, to receive my flight details and confirm with my school, United World College US, of my acceptance and itinerary via email. One decade (and a half) later, I am using technology including artificial intelligence to retell, own and share Africa's stories, ideas and innovations with the world for this generation and the next. Technology is truly a tool for progress towards a better society and Africa has always and will always be innovating, as a mother does for the survival of her daughters and sons.

Ancestors' Voices, Echoes and Wisdom
@panafricanquote

"What I call middle-class society is any society that becomes rigidified in predetermined forms, forbidding all evolution, all gains, all progress, all discovery. I call middle-class a closed society in which life has no taste, in which the air is tainted, in which ideas and men are

corrupt. And I think that a man who takes a stand against this death is in a sense a revolutionary." - Frantz Fanon

"Revolutions are brought about by men, by men who think as men of action and act as men of thought." - Kwame Nkrumah

"We are fighting for the noblest cause on earth, the liberation of mankind....there is only one race, the human race. Multi-racialism is racism multiplied." - Robert Sebukwe

"The land is ours. It's not European and we have taken it, we have given it to the rightful people... Those of white extraction who happen to be in the country and are farming are welcome to do so, but they must do so on the basis of equality." - Robert Mugabe

"Africa will write its own history, and it will be, to the north and to the south of the Sahara, a history of glory and dignity." - Patrice Lumumba

"The African people are the PAC and the PAC is the African people." - John Nyathi Pokela

"African nationalism is meaningless, dangerous, anachronistic, if it is not, at the same time, pan-Africanism." - Julius K. Nyerere

"I shall continue to insist that our sovereign countries work to achieve the United States of Africa." - Muammar al-Gaddafi

"If we maintain a certain amount of caution and organization we deserve victory....You cannot carry out fundamental change without a certain amount of madness. In this case, it comes from nonconformity, the courage to turn your back on the old formulas, the courage to invent the future." - Thomas Sankara

"In the past, we spoke of poverty, misery only in the south. Now there is a lot of misery, a lot of bad that creates victims in the north as well. This has become manifest: the global system was not made to serve the good of all, but to serve multinational companies." - Ahmed Ben Bella

"We're a sentimental people. We like a few kind words better than millions of dollars given in a humiliating way." - Gamal Abdel Nasser

"Always bear in mind that people are not fighting for ideas, for the things in anyone's head. They are fighting to win material benefits, to live better and in peace, to see their lives go forward, to guarantee the future of their children." - Amilcar Cabral

"The Black skin is not a badge of shame, but rather a glorious symbol of national greatness." - Marcus Garvey

"The job of a revolutionary is, of course, to overthrow unjust systems and replace them with just systems because a revolutionary understands this can only be done by the masses of the people. So, the task of the revolutionary is to organize the masses of the people, given the conditions of the Africans around the world who are disorganized, consequently all my efforts are going to organizing people." - Kwame Toure

"When the Missionaries arrived, the Africans had the Land and the Missionaries had the Bible. They taught us how to pray with our eyes closed. When we opened them, they had the land and we had the Bible." - Jomo Kenyatta

"The central objective in decolonising the African mind is to overthrow the authority which alien traditions

exercise over the African. This demands the dismantling of white supremacist beliefs, and the structures which uphold them, in every area of African life. It must be stressed, however, that decolonisation does not mean ignorance of foreign traditions; it simply means denial of their authority and withdrawal of allegiance from them." - Chinweizu Ibekwe

"My heart yearns for an Africa that is no more, but I shall labour for a new, free, independent and sovereign Africa that shall be respected by nations of the world." - Muziwakhe Limbede

"The thing to do is to get organized; keep separated and you will be exploited, you will be robbed, you will be killed. Get organized and you will compel the world to respect you." - Marcus Garvey

"Capitalism is a development by refinement from feudalism, just as feudalism is development by refinement from slavery ... Capitalism is but the gentlemen's method of slavery." - Kwame Nrumah

"For a colonized people the most essential value, because the most concrete, is first and foremost the land: the land which will bring them bread and, above all, dignity." - Frantz Fanon

"As a people, our most cherished and valuable achievements are the achievements of spirit. With an Afrocentric spirit, all things can be made to happen; it is the source of genuine revolutionary commitment." - Dr. Molefi Kete Asante

"Our wounds are too fresh and too painful still for us to drive them from our memory. We have known harassing work, exacted in exchange for salaries which did not permit us to eat enough to drive away hunger, or to clothe ourselves, or to house ourselves decently, or to raise our children as creatures dear to us." - Patrice Lumumba

"Our wounds are too fresh and too painful still for us to drive them from our memory. We have known harassing work, exacted in exchange for salaries which did not permit us to eat enough to drive away hunger, or to clothe ourselves, or to house ourselves decently, or to raise our children as creatures dear to us." - Patrice Lumumba

"Capitalism means that the masses will work, and a few people — who may not labor at all — will benefit from that work. The few will sit down to a banquet, and the masses will eat whatever is left over." - Julius Nyerere

"We of Africa protest that, in this day and age, we should continue to be treated as lesser human beings than other races." - Robert Mugabe

"Let me plead with you, lovers of my Africa, to carry with you into the world the vision of a new Africa." - Robert Sobukwe

"We must, therefore, appreciate our role. We must appreciate our responsibility. The African people have entrusted their whole future to us. And we have sworn that we are leading them, not to death, but to life abundant." - Robert Sobukwe

"The philosophy of Africanism holds out the hope of a genuine democracy beyond the stormy sea of struggle." - Robert Sobukwe

"Africa is one continent, one people, and one nation." - Kwame Nkrumah

"The power of the white world is threatened whenever a black man refuses to accept the white world's definitions." - James Baldwin

"At the bottom of education, at the bottom of politics, even at the bottom of religion, there must be for our race economic independence." - Booker T Washington

"I am not going to leave this land. I will die as a martyr at the end." - Col. Muammar al-Gaddafi

"The traditional face of Africa includes an attitude towards man which can only be described as being socialist." - Kwame Nkrumah

"It is better to die for an idea that will live than to live for an idea that will die." - Onkgopotse Tiro

"The wheel of progress revolves relentlessly and all the nations of the world take their turn at the field-glass of human destiny. Africa will not retreat! Africa will not compromise! Africa will not relent! Africa will not equivocate! And she will be heard! Remember Africa!" - Robert Sobukwe

"Here is a tree rooted in African soil, nourished with waters from the rivers of Afrika. Come and sit under its shade and become, with us, the leaves of the same branch and the branches of the same tree." - Robert Sobukwe

"While revolutionaries as individuals can be murdered, you cannot kill ideas." - Thomas Sankara

"Who will ever forget the massacres where so many of our brothers perished..." - Thomas Sankara

"We, in Africa, have no more need of being 'converted' to socialism than we have of being 'taught' democracy. Both are rooted in our past — in the traditional society which produced us." - Julius Nyerere

"To take part in the African revolution it is not enough to write a revolutionary song; you must fashion the revolution with the people." - Sekou Toure

"We take our stand on the principle that Afrika is one and desires to be one and nobody, I repeat, nobody has the right to balkanise our land." - Robert Sobukwe

"A people without the knowledge of their past history, origin and culture is like a tree without roots." - Marcus Garvey

"We are witnesses today of cold and calculated brutality and bestiality, the desperate attempts of a dying generation to stay in power." - Robert Sobukwe

"Personalities and fame pass; the revolution must remain." - Samora Machel

"We are no longer going to ask for the land, but we are going to take it without negotiating." - Robert Mugabe

"As far as I am concerned, I am in the knowledge that death can never extinguish the torch which I have lit in Ghana and Africa. Long after I am dead and gone, the light will continue to burn and be borne aloft, giving light and guidance to all people." - Kwame Nkrumah

"International solidarity is not an act of charity: It is an act of unity between allies fighting on different terrains toward the same objective. The foremost of these objectives is to aid the development of humanity to the highest level possible." - Samora Machel

"Throughout history, it has been the inaction of those who could have acted, the indifference of those who should have known better, the silence of the voice of justice when it mattered most, that has made it possible for evil to triumph." - Hailie Selasie I

"If we, are to remain free, if we are to enjoy the full benefit of Africa's resources, we must be united to plan for our total defense and the full exploitation of our

material and human means in the full interest of all our people. To go it alone will limit our horizons, curtail our expectations and threaten our liberty." - Kwame Nkrumah

"We regard it as the sacred duty of every African state to strive ceaselessly and energetically for the creation of a United States of Africa from Cape to Cairo and Madagascar to Morocco." - Robert Sobukwe

"There is no time to waste. We must either unite now or perish." - Julius Nyerere

"Let the free people of the world know that we could have bargained over and sold out our cause in return for a personal secure and stable life. We received many offers to this effect but we chose to be at the vanguard of the confrontation as a badge of duty and honour." - Muammar al-Gaddafi

"We have said we will never collapse, never ever. We may have our droughts, our poverty, but as a people we shall never collapse, never ever." - Robert Mugabe

"One who wants to create a future must not forget the past." - Muziwakhe Limbede

"Educate ourselves; educate other people, the population in general, to fight fear and ignorance, to eliminate little by little the subjection to nature and natural forces which our economy has not yet mastered." - Amilcar Cabral

"Until all Africans stand and speak as free human beings, equal in the eyes of the Almighty; until that day, the African continent shall not know peace." - Haile Selassie I

"I don't lead terrorists. I lead Africans who want their self-government and land. God did not intend that one nation be ruled by another forever." - Dedan Kimathi

"We are proud of this struggle, of tears, of fire, and of blood, to the depths of our being, for it was a noble and just struggle, and indispensable to put an end to the humiliating slavery which was imposed upon us by force." - Patrice Lumumba

"Our children may learn about the heroes of the past. Our task is to make ourselves the architects of the future." - Jomo Kenyatta

"Our main armament was not guns but words–thousands and thousands of words, written and

spoken to rally our people, to lay our claims before the British Government and the world, to express our anger and frustration at the denial of our birthright to rule our own country." - Kenneth Kaunda

"The struggle of the African people is more noble than the eagle on the American dollar." - Zephania Mothopeng

"Our efforts to promote continental integration must place education of our people at the top of our priorities, as key elements in addressing development challenges." - Sam Nujoma

"We wish to be the heirs of all the revolutions of the world, of all the liberation struggles of the peoples of the Third World." - Thomas Sankara

"I want to salute the Kenyan voters on one other issue – the rejection of the blackmail by the International Criminal Court (ICC) and those who seek to abuse this institution for their own agenda." - Yoweri Kaguta Museveni

"People go to Africa and confirm what they already have in their heads and so they fail to see what is there in front of them." - Chinua Achebe

"The African Union may be a shadow of the original post-colonial vision. But its potential to inspire remains." - Ngugi wa Thiong'o

"Africa can and will only advance through African integration, which can be realized through the Federal United States of Africa." - Cheikh Anta Diop

"Colonialists stole not only the lands of African people and renamed them. They stole also their knowledge, so that they would know nothing about themselves." - Motsoko Pheko

"It is important to nurture any new ideas and initiatives which can make a difference for Africa." - Wangari Maathai

"Our contribution has to be given not only for the liquidation of the colonial system but also for the liquidation of ignorance, disease and primitive forms of social organization." - Agostinho Neto

"We shall defend our freedom and independence to the last drop of our blood." - Gamal Abdel Nasser

"If our people lose the courage to confront what is wrong then we become collaborators." - Jerry Rawlings

"Let us all agree to die a little, or even completely so that African unity may not be a vain word." - Ahmed Ben Bella

"Africans a-liberate Zimbabwe; Every man got a right to decide his own destiny..." - Bob Marley

"Being black is not a matter of pigmentation – being black is a reflection of a mental attitude." - Steve Biko

"We paid the ultimate price for it and we are determined never to relinquish our sovereignty and remain masters of our destiny. Zimbabwe will never be a colony again." - Robert Mugabe

"The enemies of a people are those who keep them in ignorance." - Thomas Sankara

"To ensure national unity, there must be no Shonas in Zimbabwe, there must be no Ndebeles in Zimbabwe, there must be Zimbabweans. Some people are proud of their tribalism. But we call tribalists reactionary agents of the enemy." - Samora Machel

"It is better to die for an idea that will live, than to live for an idea that will die." - Steve Biko

"For Africa to me… is more than a glamorous fact. It is a historical truth. No man can know where he is going unless he knows exactly where he has been and exactly how he arrived at his present place." - Maya Angelou

"Africa needs back its economy, its politics, its culture, its languages and all its patriotic writers." - Ngugi wa Thiong'o

"Never be shamed of being Afrikan." - Thomas Sankara

"Africa is the Spiritual Frontier of human kind." - W. E. B. DuBois

"We are anti-nobody. We are pro-Africa. We breathe, we dream, we live Africa; because African and humanity are inseparable." - Robert Sobukwe

"We are living today, Sons and Daughters of the Soil, fighters in the cause of African freedom, in an era that is pregnant with untold possibilities for good and evil." - Robert Sobukwe

"Politically we stand for government of the Africans for the Africans by the Africans, with everybody who owes his loyalty only to Africa and accepts the- democratic rule of an African majority, being regarded as an African." - Robert Sobukwe

"Forces of white supremacy are in retreat before the irresistible march of African nationalism. This is the era of African emancipation. Africa holds the stage today." - Robert Sobukwe

"The masses of the people of Africa are crying for unity. The people of Africa call for the breaking down of the boundaries that keep them apart." - Kwame Nkrumah

"We do not want any more agitation, any more disorder, any more pointless words, any more slogans. The only slogan for the moment must be, economic progress." - Patrice Lumumba

"There can be no black-white unity until there is first some black unity.... We cannot think of uniting with others, until after we have first united among ourselves. We cannot think of being acceptable to others until we have first proven acceptable to ourselves." - Malcom X

"Africa's story has been written by others; we need to own our problems and solutions and write our story." - Paul Kagame

"The great powers of the world may have done wonders in giving the world an industrial and military look but the great gift still has to come from Africa – giving the world a more human face." - Steve Biko

"Africa is our center of gravity, our cultural and spiritual mother and father, our beating heart, no matter where we live on the face of this earth." - John Henrik Clarke

"We must learn to live the African way. It's the only way to live in freedom and with dignity." - Thomas Sankara

"Our grandfathers had to run, run, run. My generation's out of breath. We ain't running no more." - Kwame Toure

"A race that is solely dependent upon another for economic existence sooner or later dies." - Marcus Garvey

"The Church in the colonies is the white people's Church, the foreigner's Church. She does not call the

native to God's ways but to the ways of the white man, of the master, of the oppressor." - Frantz Fanon

"Children of Robert Mangaliso Sobukwe, Finish what you have started. Children of Robert Mugabe,finish what you have started." - Xola Skosana

"We do not want to be reminded that it is we, the indigenous people, who are poor and exploited in the land of our birth." - Steve Biko

"The conqueror writes history, they came, they conquered and they write. You don't expect the people who came to invade us to tell the truth about us." - Miriam Makeba

"You can't have Capitalism without Racism." - Malcom X

"We meet here today, to rededicate ourselves to the cause of Afrika, to establish contact beyond the grave, with the great African heroes and assure them that their struggle was not in vain." - Robert Sobukwe

"We are fighting for our land and that land is still in the hands of the oppressor. In other words the struggle can't stop until we attain our goal." - Clarence Makwetu

"The revolution and women's liberation go together. We do not talk of women's emancipation as an act of charity or out of a surge of human compassion. It is a basic necessity for the revolution to triumph. Women hold up the other half of the sky." - Thomas Sankara

"Our fathers fought bravely. But do you know the biggest weapon unleashed by the enemy against them? It was not the Maxim gun. It was division among them. Why? Because a people united in faith are stronger than the bomb." - Ngugi wa Thiong'o

"Decolonisation is the total eradication of colonial legacies; this cannot be done on a judicial level. We merely uphold the Constitution. The work will happen through the grassroots..." - Dikgang Moseneke

"Cassius Clay is a name that white people gave to my slave master. Now that I am free, that I don't belong anymore to anyone, that I'm not a slave anymore, I gave back their white name, and I chose a beautiful African one." - Muhammad Ali

"We know that Africa is neither French, nor British, nor American, nor Russian, that it is African." - Patrice Lumumba

"The role of students in our universities is to proclaim the truth at all times irrespective of the consequences thereof. they should realise that it is their bounden duty to address themselves to black people and to show them the way to freedom without flinching." - Zephania Mothopeng

PART 1: Once Upon A Time – The Advent of Mankind

The Human Journey DNA (Source: National Geographic)

Chapter 1: Mankind's Cradle – Caveman, Early Art, Hunters, Gatherers and Fire

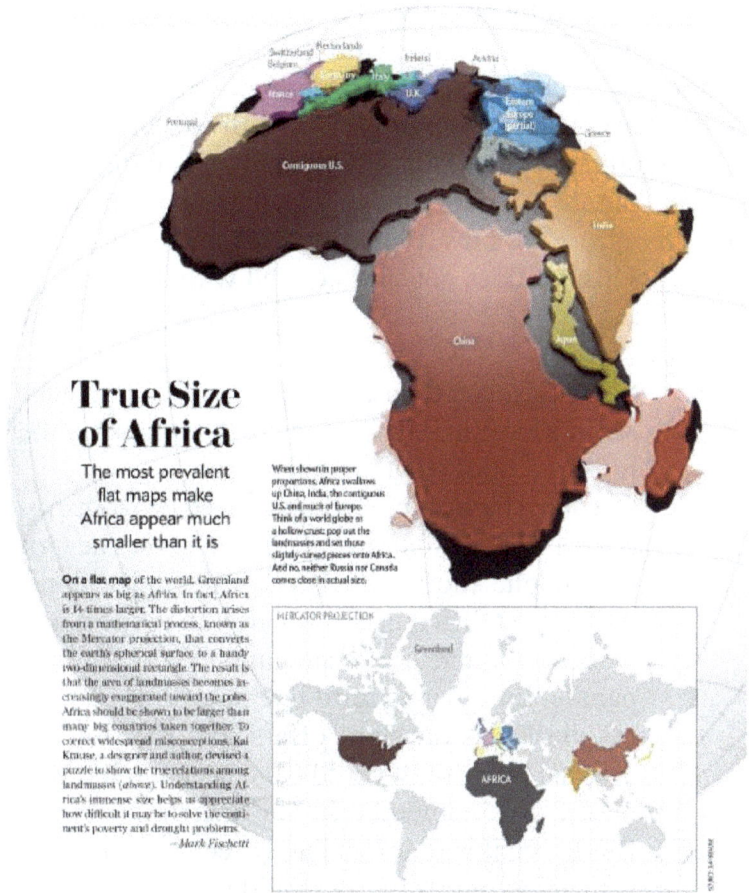

True Size of Africa

The most prevalent flat maps make Africa appear much smaller than it is

When shown in proper proportions, Africa swallows up China, India, the contiguous U.S. and much of Europe. Think of a world globe as a hollow crust: pop out the landmasses and set those slightly-curved pieces onto Africa. And no, neither Russia nor Canada comes close in actual size.

On a flat map of the world, Greenland appears as big as Africa. In fact, Africa is 14-times larger. The distortion arises from a mathematical process, known as the Mercator projection, that converts the earth's spherical surface to a handy two-dimensional rectangle. The result is that the area of landmasses becomes increasingly exaggerated toward the poles. Africa should be shown to be larger than many big countries taken together. To correct widespread misconceptions, Kai Krause, a designer and author, devised a puzzle to show the true relations among landmasses (above). Understanding Africa's immense size helps us appreciate how difficult it may be to solve the continent's poverty and drought problems.
— *Mark Fischetti*

Needed: Media Representation of Africa as a Global Giant

"Once upon a time there was…," are words in over 2000 African languages and dialects passed down from memory, generation to generation. The words are often followed by narratives, some real some fiction, others mythical or hybrids with the singular purpose of informing, entertaining and educating. Africa's history indeed is not singular in origin but as diverse as its multicultural people. Thus I will not dwell on this, but rather capture the main innovations that helped mankind progress from cave dwelling to settling and nomadism. Africa's history does not start nor end with colonial slavery.

Seventy-seven thousand years ago, a craftsman sat in a cave in a limestone cliff overlooking the rocky coast of what is now the Indian Ocean...The man picked up a piece of reddish brown stone about three inches long that he—or she, no one knows—had polished. With a stone point, he etched a geometric design in the flat surface—simple cross hatchings framed by two parallel lines with a third line down the middle.Today the stone offers no clue to its original purpose. It could have been a religious object, an ornament or just an ancient doodle. But to see it is to immediately recognize it as something only a person could have made. Carving the stone was a very human thing to do. Henshilwood, an archaeologist at Norway's University of Bergen and the University of the Witwatersrand, in South Africa, found the carving on land owned by his grandfather, near the southern tip of the African continent.

When the study of human origins intensified in the 20th century, two main theories emerged to explain the archaeological and fossil record: one, known as the multi-regional hypothesis, suggested that a species of human ancestor dispersed throughout the globe, and modern humans evolved from this predecessor in several different locations. The other, out-of-Africa theory, held that modern humans evolved in Africa for many thousands of years before they spread throughout the rest of the world. When the migration was complete, Homo sapiens was the last—and only—man standing.

Mitochondrial DNA is inherited only from the mother. About 200,000 years ago, a woman existed whose mitochondrial DNA was the source of the mitochondrial DNA in every person alive today. That is, all of us are her descendants. Scientists call her "Eve." This is something of a misnomer, for Eve was neither the first modern human nor the only woman alive 200,000 years ago. But she did live at a time when the modern human population was small—about 10,000 people, according to one estimate. She is the only woman from that time to have an unbroken lineage of daughters, though she is neither our only ancestor nor our oldest ancestor. She is, instead, simply our "most recent common ancestor," at least when it comes to mitochondria. Eve, mitochondrial DNA backtracking showed, lived in Africa.

As the gaps are filled, the story is likely to change, but in broad outline, today's scientists believe that from their beginnings in Africa, modern humans went first to Asia between 80,000 and 60,000 years ago. By 45,000 years ago, or possibly earlier, they had settled in Indonesia, Papua New Guinea and Australia. The moderns entered Europe around 40,000 years ago, probably via two routes: from Turkey along the Danube corridor into eastern Europe, and along the Mediterranean coast. By 35,000 years ago, they were firmly established in most of the Old World. The Neanderthals, forced into mountain strongholds in Croatia, the Iberian Peninsula, the Crimea and elsewhere, would become extinct 25,000 years ago. Finally, around 15,000 years ago, humans crossed from Asia to North America and from there to South America.

...one day in 1999, anthropologist Alan Morris of South Africa's University of Cape Town showed Frederick Grine, a visiting colleague from Stony Brook University, an unusual-looking skull on his bookcase. Morris told Grine that the skull had been discovered in the 1950s at Hofmeyr, in South Africa. Thirty-six thousand years ago, says

Grine, Morris, before the world's human population differentiated into the mishmash of races and ethnicities that exist today, "We were all Africans." [Guy Gugliotta for The Smithsonian]

Since the 1990 a consensus has grown that modern humans emerged in Africa at least 20,000 years ago. This shift in thinking began in 1987. Using genetic analysis to construct an evolutionary tree of mitochondrial DNA-genetic material we inherit solely from our ancestry back to a single woman who lived in East Africa some 200,000 to 150,000 years ago - the-so-called "mitochondrial Eve" [Human Origins pg 97].

Thus with mankind's origin established and more discoveries adding years to the original migration dates out of Africa, the African must remain proud and nurture the motherland, a responsibility that starts with hunters and gatherers 200,000 years ago or more today. The hunter and gatherers are already innovative leveraging the fundamental definition of technology as that which allows one to perform work or an activity faster or better than before. As taught by my Lafayette College Policy Professor Benjamin Cohen, technology is a neutral (neither inherently good nor bad) means to an end and not the end itself (and need not necessarily be inevitable).

The African (the modern human as some archaeologists may say) already has innovative tools for hunting such as shard rocks and sticks, is aware of his environment and adapts to it from relying on caves or Oasis and fishing among other activities. Most important though is also the understanding of Africans' creative insight and exploration, from the cave paintings to rock carvings and other art forms. This visual and physical form of communication, storytelling and record keeping is complemented by oral or audio storytelling; a great foundation for an innovative society.

The Southern population innovations are not so independent from the Northern, Western, Central and Eastern populations within Africa, only varying to adapt to the local environment. Fishing, gathering of tropical fruits and food as well as hunting of game local to each area provide the critical sustenance needed for the communities. The nile water feeds the North as much as the Niger river feeds the West and the Indian Ocean feeds the East providing sustenance for both land and sea life and a great system of ecological interdependence.

Nomadism evolves as a way to mitigate conflicts, explore new areas as well as escape natural disasters and outbreaks. Despite all this, Africa's warm weather provides the best environment for food, varied innovations and migrations. As populations grow, some communities stay longer in some areas and develop customs and rituals unique to those areas of settlement. This is evident from the remains of bones without flesh or heads removed for ceremonial or ritual purposes and cave paintings capturing some of these celebrations as seen in most modern museums as well as the Egyptian tombs.

Important to clarify too is the use of fire in various activities and processes from bush clearing to cooking and ultimately security. The size of the fire varies depending on the time, location and use case. Logs are the initial use, though later scenarios have fish oil/fat remnants being used. Animal hide transformation to clothing and other bedding material is already established here. Further innovations are early stage pottery along the Nile and craftsmanship such as use of shells from the sea for ornaments and necklaces among other items.

The early versions of boats and ships are seen as early as the Modern Human's migration from Africa towards the rest of the world. It is the fundamental innovations of food gathering tools like baskets and spears, preparation with knives and pots and preservation such as granaries of salting as well as adaptability in the use of fire for security and ultimately harnessing animals and boats for transport that elevate migration patterns and enable the great exodus from Africa to the European, Asian and Arabic territories.

Chapter 2: Before Mesopotamia – Original Nile Civilizations, East and West Africa

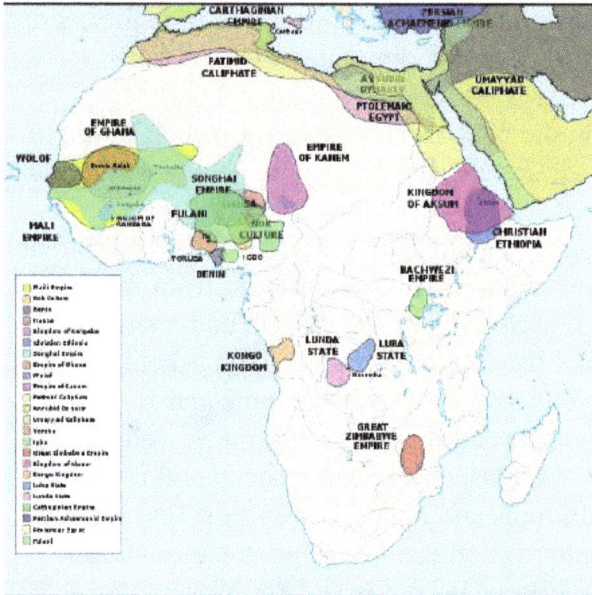

Once Upon a Time: African Populations (Source: Wikimedia)

Migration and settlement have been constant and evolving phases across Africa both for basic survival and ultimately for adventure and need to establish new communities. The organic and often unstructured patterns may be confusing to the outsider but the intra Africa migrations often follow an earlier phase of settlement as well as cross cultural interaction unless they are dictated by natural disasters like disease and famine.

Nowhere is the value of rich arable land/soil, water and good climate to settlements more visible than along the Nile River, the longest river in Africa. River Nile gives birth to the earliest and longest settlements across Africa. the Nilotics (people of the Nile) emerge from these settlements and support later migrations. The Nile also nurtures the great Egyptian dynasties and kingdoms. It is said through folk stories that civilization started along the Nile.

From modern farming techniques like irrigation to health/urban innovations like drainage canals in towns and cities and architecture marvels like the pyramids, the Nile becomes a source of inspiration, sustenance and stability for those who live around it. The water, flowing Northwards from Uganda to the mediterranean connects cultures and communities both via land and water enabling agriculture and later trade and settlements at scale.

Similar settlements are seen along the southern tip of Africa, in the Northern areas of Morocco and along the East African costs. The Western areas around the Niger river also foster settlements and growth of rain dependent crops like nuts, large scale fishing and other activities.

It is the development of iron smelting and the resulting iron tools like pangas, spears, arrows and other resources like cooking pans, plates or knives that accelerates both settlements and migrations. The new iron tools not only support farming and agriculture to support longer periods of settlement but also larger communities as seen along the Nile.

The tools also allow development of military or defence weaponry unique to the communities. Granaries are dug or constructed for storage while fences are built to secure the communities. Socially, the leaderships evolve from small households to chiefdoms and ultimately kingdoms.

It is also along the Nile that the papyrus plays a critical role in record keeping and education, serving as the source for paper or writing material. Rocks, walls, clothes and weapons compliment these innovations often carrying visual or symbolic records, statements and histories. This visual script is seen across Egypt, the Houssa in Western Africa and even the cave paintings and ornaments from the Eastern to the Southern regions of Africa.

Drums, flutes, calabashes and other instruments are created to bring African music and poetry to light. Settlements lead to customs and rituals around birth, death, names, harvests, weddings or marriage, burial, war, peace, welcoming or leaving a community. It is migration within Africa that leads to even more inter-cultural mixes, enrichment and evolution both socially and politically to the developed Africa that later becomes the envy of the world.

African migrations and movements are as old as the settlements across Africa but oral histories and mythology capture most of the fundamental migration movements and the reasons for that. At the core is the usual flight from natural disasters or conflict complimented by a genuine desire for adventure and conquests by other communities. This is made easier with the invention of tools and resources like iron smelting that allow communities to recreate instruments from memory and not be burdened with carrying everything from place to place. Priority is given to agriculture, security, communication, health and cultural rituals including music for most of the early innovations. Culture and its role grows fundamentally over time as both a strategic tactic to immerse new communities within one's own cultural ways or as a tool for diplomacy and trade across communities.

Chapter 3: Royal Legacy - Migration for Language, Arts and Culture Development

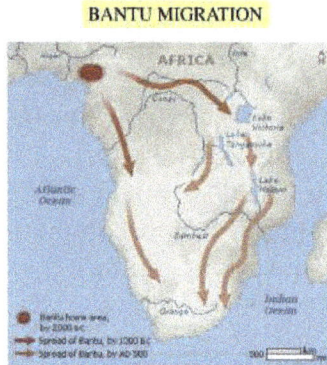

BANTU MIGRATION

Encarta

The Bantu Migration, Intra-Africa for Economic Growth and Security (Source: Encarta Software)

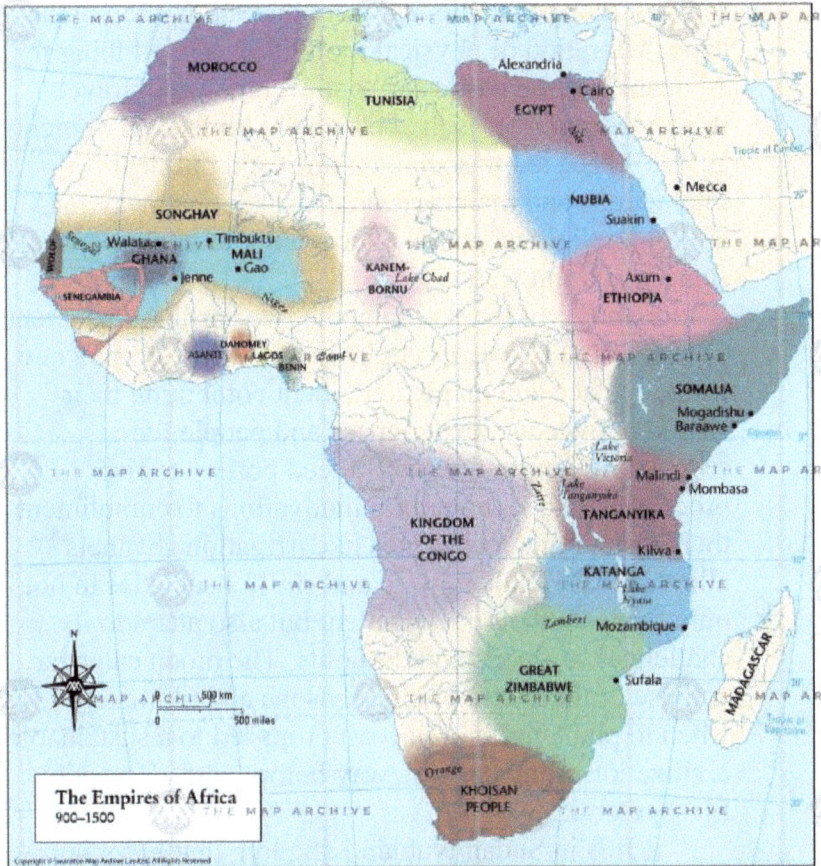

Resulting Empires from Bantu Migration Adapt and Thrive. (Source: The Map Archive)

The migration, from cradle to current areas is best illustrated by three migration theories: the west to central migration, the Nile to the East and South migration and the South to the East and Central migration. Migrations starts around the West Africa regions, along the Nile and from the South, the Southern cape. Migration or physical mobility is a good thing for Africans and the world for "one who does not travel thinks their mother is the best cook." Indeed movements across Africa led to social, cultural and political interactions and maintained a consistent pathway for cultural, religious, philosophical and political knowledge sharing and innovations.

In Egypt for example, the two earliest settlements of Upper and Lower Egypt later combine to form a new capital/palace and major settlement combining their shared knowledge, experiences and people for a sustainable future. From advanced pottery to fish processing and architectural innovations to compliment their agriculture, techniques like irrigation channels allowed these ancient, wise and skillful societies to not only navigate their environment but also adapt to its challenges of floods and droughts. The moon calendar, and use of the sun to predict seasons and ultimately when to plant, grow or harvest crops led to a sustainable civilization along the Nile way before, and alongside Mesopotamia.

It is in Sudan/Nubian Kingdom that Egyptian influence spreads, from complimenting their pyramid building to knowledge sharing of mathematical discoveries like numbers, visual writing, papyrus, and date system or calendars. Sudan's civilizations evolve to the Nilotics who are the ancestors to a large group of Eastern and Southern Africans thanks to migration. The Nilotics belong to the Bantu group, the largest intra Africa demographic and migration. Across East and

Southern Africa and to some extent Central Africa, the Nilotics influence and impact persists to date.

While migrations are in search of better land, water or opportunities, as settlements become bigger and evolve, some are due to leadership battles, internal conflicts or an expansionist mindset, driven by a need to connect with other African groups, conquer or assimilate and ultimately spread their influence and knowledge. Iron smelting, and agriculture knowledge as well as food preservation techniques relying on the sun and salt allow for longer travels and movements with military weapons from arrows to spears and jembes/pangas as well as axes and sicles for grass and land clearing. Depending on the culture (nomadic or settlement driven), minimal constructions or permanent forts and settlements are constructed to allow the newly integrated groups to defend, sustain and grow their influence.

Culturally for most societies and demographics, there is a patriarchy and leadership follows a hereditary or birth right process as is the same for succession and inheritance policies and customs. Marriage, birth and death celebrations and rituals evolve and are passed down generation after generation, varying with intermarriages among different demographics. Marriage also becomes a way to sustain peace and bolster alliances between conflicting communities. There is great evidence of this among the areas along the East African coast where the Southern Africa to North and the Bantu migrations from the Nile and West Africa intersect. Here the people challenge each other for political, social and cultural assimilations and intermarriages as well as political strategies driven by a need to grow communities in numbers become a way to foster co-existence. It becomes apparent through conflict and war that larger communities can withstand war or external conflicts, natural disasters and have sufficient labor force for agriculture, defence and cultural development. It is the Zulu in the South who are one of the successful societies in assimilating and influencing other cultures and customs to theirs from the Southern tip of Southern Africa to the Great Lakes region of East Africa.

In addition to the technical and political knowledge shared across generations and communities, there is also evolution of language, arts and religion. For example, each society has an origin story, often told through oral mythology with symbolic ornaments, animals and other natural symbols to give visual memory to the origin story. As such some trees, animals and natural elements like hills, valleys have unique and sacred meaning to some societies. From the sun in Egypt to the snake or cow and lion in some Bantu societies, nature is intertwined with humanity's existence. Indeed to this day, the black panther still echoes its mystery and relevance across the East African region and around the world blending reality and fiction but also continuing the old told tradition of African ancestry rooted in secrecy, mystery and symbolism as a way to create, disseminate and protect community intelligence and wisdom. Storytelling mostly oral takes on a critical role of capturing a people's history, their ancestry, journey, heroes, beliefs, customs and dreams.

As populations rise fostered by improved tool making with iron smelting and agriculture with irrigation, as well as food preservation with sun drying, salting and silos or granary storage, societies are able to settle for longer periods and evolve culturally, politically as well as economically. Armies for example evolve from sticks and rocks to infantry and cavalry ranks as well as elite mercenaries and royalty bodyguards. Settlements also lead to formal education and libraries as well as evolution of barter trade and ultimately seal/signatory (from the chiefs and kings) driven transactions such as food rations, loot allocations from battle, promotions and inter community agreements or diplomacy.

Hierarchies around chiefdoms and kingdoms allow for both specialization and shared visions and destinies among community members with each contributing their best. From farmers to iron smelters to fighters and legislators, Africans develop and evolve their democratic practices through community courts, open forums and court systems. Individual or family votes articulate a people's values, concerns and expectations which regents, chiefs, emissaries and leaders respect and implement. Due to the awareness of both external challenges like war or internal like coups or natural disasters like diseases and famine, communities develop best practices including establishment of spy networks that infiltrate other communities for intelligence gathering, counter intelligence and advance warning. Family relatives in intermarriage families are put to use serving their own or the assimilated communities.

Barter trade, a value based exchange system develops and spreads across Africa as an accepted form as chiefdoms and kingdoms grow or are established. Grains, meat, textiles like the Bark Cloth (clothes from the bark of a special tree in the Buganda kingdom, a Bantu tribe) create specialization in some communities such as nomads focusing on animal husbandry and settlers on both including agriculture, processing and storage often in bulk and at scale. Meat, fish, milk, yogurt, cheese, fruits, grains and spices, teas, herbs all evolve and appreciate in value based on their scarcity, production and processing techniques and their demand across the kingdoms. Trade, in times of peace, allows societies to consume and share more than they produce, resulting in even faster knowledge and resource accumulation.

Needless to say, migrations followed by settlement make it a strategic mandate for chiefs, kings and patriarchs to plan ahead of time the ideal settlement locations for their people. The survival and future of a community indeed becomes the number one reason for succession conflicts and later kingdom wars creating a regular or cyclical pattern to the rise and fall of kingdoms across Africa i.e one's rise is often at the expense of another falling as they are expansionary in nature. But some manage to handle expansion and stability through assimilation, education and trade allowing communities to grow beyond their original dreams. Unity, peace and constant innovation become traits of empires that survive the geo-politics of the cradle of mankind.

Chapter 4: The Emperor - The Rise and Fall of Empires
(Trade, Infrastructure and Politics)

African Civilizations: Royalty and Rich Multiculturalism
(Source: Wikimedia).

*Stolen African Royal and Cultural Records sit in
Western Museums (Source: Wikimedia).*

Visual storytelling in ancient Egypt. Colonialists started with extraction of such art, culture and monuments to erase and rewrite African History (Source: Wikimedia).

The same social, political and economic challenges that led to migration also support or mirror the establishment and later fall of empires and monarchs albeit at different phases and stages. Like an orchestra with different notes and keys, the African empires rise and fall at different stages yet each empire's rise or fall is intertwined with others. From the Egyptian kingdoms and their pharaohs to the Nubian Kingdom, the Zulu Empire, the Buganda Kingdom in the East, Ethiopia in the Horn of Africa and Kanem Bornu Empire in Western Africa among others, Africa nurtured and thrived under its empires. Agriculture such as irrigation and farming tools, education backed by libraries like Timbuktu and Egypts papyrus writings, military training and adventures, sailing on boats, food processing and storage innovations as the key to long term survival and value addition for trade evolved as kingdoms and chiefdoms competed to outlast each other while bartering and trading and gifting in times of peace and war.

Mansa Musa of Mali is one example of Africa's wealth and like other Kings in West and North Africa, ventures across the Sahara desert to the Middle East and interacts with some leaders in Europe and Asia often bearing gifts of gold and other precious minerals. In exchange scientists, librarians and other experts are invited to come learn from Africa but also help with its economic and urban development. Timbuktu thrives under such programs, as a library city housing knowledge of world scholars from the continent and as far as the middle east. The kings surround themselves with the educated, philosophers, music and cultural experts, well travelled and experienced advisors as well as the most battle tested generals and intelligence officers. Cultural and religious diplomacy is practiced through gifting, rituals, intermarriages, education such as languages and religion like christianity in the case of Ethiopia or islamic principles in case of Morocco and Mali among others. Unlike Europe and Asia, Africa thrives with minimal religious tension as trade, cultural exchanges, open education systems and strong family ties and histories unite more than they divide. African religions based on a strong and human centered spirituality that honors our past, our ancestry while instructing and preparing us for the present and future allow Africans to not forget their values and literal value leading to strong sense of pride, self worth and empathy for mankind, African or foreign.

Perhaps it's Africa's hospitality that becomes its temporary ruin. The trips by Mansa Musa and stories of wealth and civilization let alone religious sophistication in Ethiopia among other tales inspire jealousy and greed among Europeans and a need for trade in Asians such as the Oman dynasty arriving to trade on the coast of East Africa and later so called explorers like Vasco da Gama and other british or European intelligence gatherers (explorers) and coercive emissaries (missionaries). Like all African voyages and ventures, foreign trips were Monarch approved and as such, initial trade, conflict and exchanges were between monarchs in most cases. For example, "great Britain" under the Queen's approval gave "regional franchise licenses" to certain British firms that were tasked with exploration of opportunities, extraction and exploitation of the value unlocked and ultimate monopoly of industries in their areas of operations. This is in contrast to the prevailing barter and near predictable or needs based value exchange along the East Africa coast, the mediterranean and West African coasts between Africa and the Middle East or India.

PART 2: The Second Coming – Outsiders as "Discoverers" who Fear the Unknown

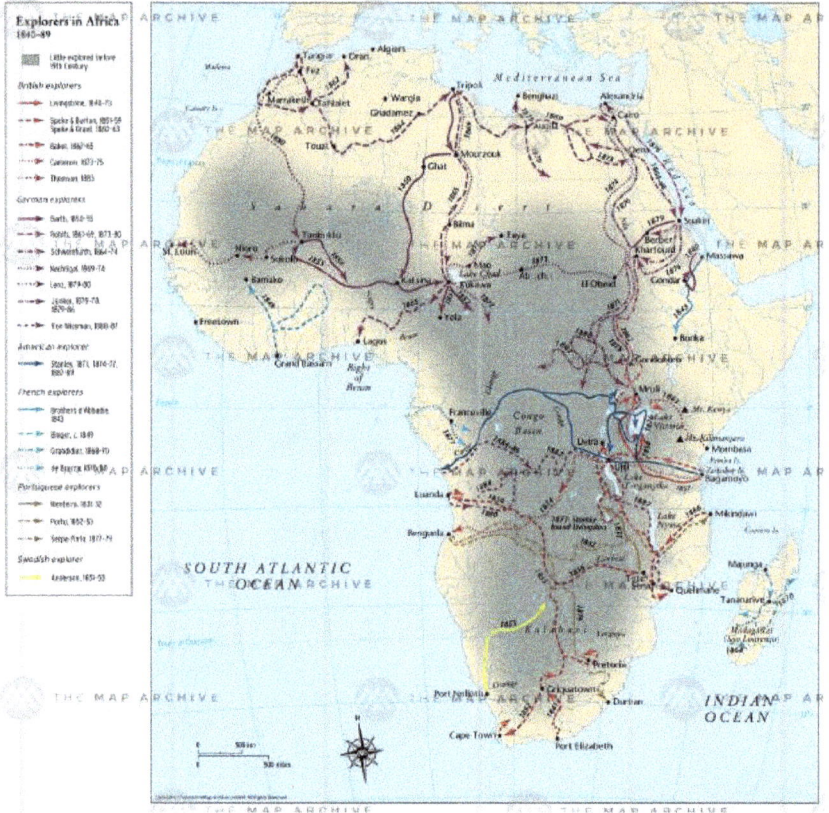

Chapter 5: East – The Rise of Value for Exchange - Middle Eastern Trade Interest in Africa

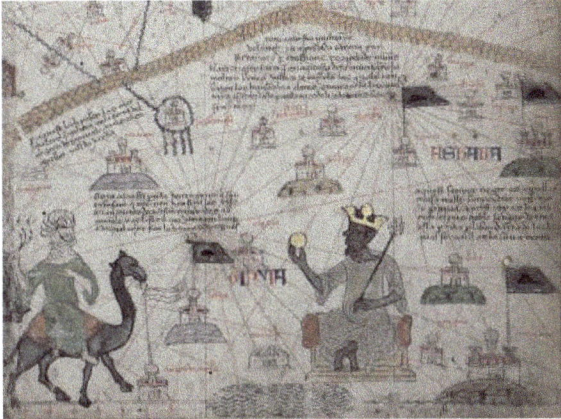

The picture of Musa holding a gold ingot in Catalan Atlas in 1375. (Source: Wikimedia)

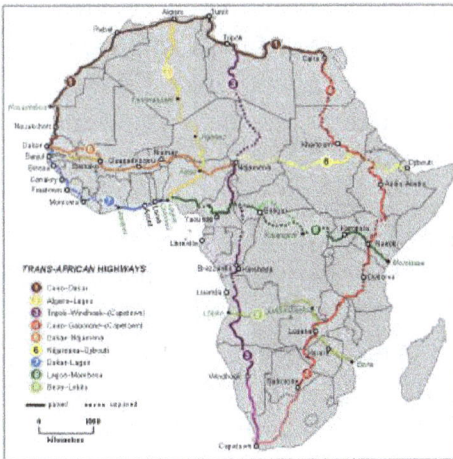

Economy of Africa: Overlap of current trading routes and hubs with ancient links like Mombasa. (Source: Wikimedia)

To understand the value, vast wealth and untapped potential across Africa, one must look at the great intra Africa migrations such as the bantu migrations that lead populations and communities to the most arable lands, mineral rich areas as well as strategic locations like ports, rivers and lakes or oasis in the North (Sahara desert) and South (Kalahari desert). Iron, gold, copper, diamonds and other minerals are extracted and used across Africa within ceremonies, trade, rituals and even architecture.

The rise and fall of kingdoms across Africa following the intra Africa migrations and settlements creates dominant trade routes, links and markets or ports. Taxes along trade routes by chiefs and kings generate a source of wealth while others die or fall in defence of these strategic locations and economic links. Ethiopia for example grows, uninterrupted for decades/centuries often venturing to the world when it needs to but never being too open to foreigners and traders unlike coastal towns and cities like Mombasa and Madagascar.

It is in the 1500 B.C or earlier that Indian/Asian traders arrive on the East African coast with a goal to trade and establish diplomatic links and allies. Their ships are the Dhows (lateen-rigged ships with one or two masts) and the routes are risky but rewarding. African's especially the Bantu along the Eastern Coast are welcoming and a result of intermarriages between Arabs and Bantu, a new language Swahili evolves rooted in Bantu language but with added arabic origin words. This language also facilitates communication, trade and relations between Africa and Asia/Middle East. the sultans send more trade and diplomatic emissaries to establish courts and residences and manage accounts along these strategic ports and trade routes along the Indian Ocean. Spices, textiles, weaponry, books, medicine and other goods are exchanged and food items introduced.

Towns and cities often with stone and brick architecture thrive along the coast, fortified against the tide and external attacks from pirates and mercenaries. Political power shifts from inland to the coast and sultans and other chiefs establish dominance and territories. Treaties are signed and taxes negotiated and urban planning implemented to facilitate future expansion and growth while inland kingdoms and communities send trade and diplomatic emissaries to the coast to trade, strike deals and participate in this value based exchange that is mostly barter. Here the trade routes, markets and links grow.

Not everyone wants to pay taxes and occasionally well guarded tradesmen over run the monarchs tax agents or launch a counter attack to control the kingdom. The trade routes become hubs for conflict but also due to a prevailing practice of assimilation or arrests (captivity for labor/slavery) the captured are gifted to the king, soldiers or traded to other traders and kings. Thus the trade routes, slowly evolve to support slave trade and mercenary hiring.

The import export trade generated intercontinental developments across Africa through trade and knowledge exchanges. While the western hyped GDP measures that often do not account for how well the populace is actually doing are not yet in circulation, at this point with barter trade along the Eastern Coast and Mediterranean, Africans seem aware of their value and wealth, negotiating great diplomatic and commercial terms with sultans and emissaries, defending ports and forts with strategic advantages as well as investing in infrastructure and processes to streamline future trade. Investments are made in education, financial training, boat/ship building and repairs as well as military training for defence and expansion of ports, palaces and the merchandise. As the ports grow and scale, they open Africa to the rest of the world and they become stop gates from Europe to Asia and India via the East, Western, Northern and Southern ports. Whereas Africans have traveled across the waters and land in earlier times to inhabit Europe, the Middle East and Asia, it took Europeans lots of tries and perfecting of their navy to finally have the confidence to risk the global voyages to the African continent. Their defeat in earlier times such as the French defeat in Egypt during the crusades or religious wars in a way give Europe a pause until they feel ready for an exploitative revenge disguised as an enlightening mission.

There is no doubt that Anthropologists continue to discover new sites, artifacts and diggings that bring into question old or known knowledge and assumptions about migration and the evolution of mankind. To date

Africa, the cradle, stands as the unanimous origin of mankind. For the rest of this book, this will be the core assumption based on years of scientific, biblical/theological and anthropological research. Africa's cultural and religious influence can be traced to Egypt and the relation to Christianity and Islam with both Moses and Jesus having found refuge in Egypt. The Ethiopian Queen Sheeba is mentioned in Genesis, the earliest book in the Bible. In the beginning, indeed, there is an interdependence of communities that learn from and influence each other unlike today's polarized and fear driven lifestyles.

Nowhere is this more clear than in Africa where the growth/rise and fall of empires and kingdoms is often linked to natural disasters, war, migration and cultural or religious influence. Mansa Moussa, the Richest/wealthiest man in the world even owns more wealth in gold, diamonds than is imaginable. His extravagant gifts and lavish generosity wherever he goes are the envy of many and bring the collapse of some economies like Egypt through inflation due to excess gold circulation. Timbuktu, Mali, a great centre of learning with libraries and schools thrives under Mansa Moussa benefiting from scholars from as far as the Middle East and Meccah. In his travels, as is the custom for most African royalty, gifts are exchanged, traders, diplomats and experts introduced but most of all invited to help the king serve his people. Scholars, architects, military trainers as well as traders return with the king to help him serve his people and develop the communities.

Mansa Moussa's wealth is estimated to be the largest in the world is a stark contrast but inspiration to today's African billionaires including Mr. Aliko Dangote (Cement, Food Processing, and Oil Refinery) and Tony Elumelu (Banking and Hospitality) among others. The success of these wealthy Africans like our ancestors Mansa Moussa, lies in their tapping into Africa's unlimited potential of natural resources, trade and diversification backed by education and or religious freedom/scholarship.

Egypt's early rise through its dynasties including Cleopatra and King Tut is complemented by the influence to Sudan's Nubia Kingdom with kings and queens treated as gods and goddesses as well as other Kingdoms like Mali empire, Kanem Bornu empire, Song Dynasty, Zulu among others. Africa's royalty establish sophisticated court systems with detailed record keeping, organization, specialization and education. These systems later help future generations organize themselves against colonialism and slavery as shown by pan Africanists as well as global Diaspora as far as Haiti against the French.

Whereas Europe and the Middle East are caught up in religious fanaticism and crusades as well as tribalism (Britain, France, Scotland etc) with orders/blessings including remission of sins(fast track to heaven) from the Pope in Rome against the "fear of muslims control of Jerusalem", Africa thrives until France's King Louis IX tries to use Egypt as a base against Islamic armies. France suffers a devastating loss as do future christian campaigns against Islam e.g the

British. Christianity at this time also thrives un interrupted by political ideologies in Ethiopia and some parts of Egypt. The European "enlightener" is in chaos fighting a fanatic religious war while Africans of all faiths (African, muslims, christian among others) co-exist, trade, learn, live and marry amongst each other.

The social, cultural, religious and political setup and institutions impact the way societies evolve or progress towards a healthier, wealthier and freer society without sacrificing independence and security. In the early days man is organized by family, villages or settlements with man as the head of the household. The families evolve from simple to extended (as these form the common lineage of tribes and languages).

The men are responsible for hunting and or gathering food such as fruits and vegetables along the way. This is in addition to fishing for those close to fresh waters or seas while women help maintain the household and societal order through cleaning, cooking, pottery, food preservation and child rearing (as a shared family/community responsibility).

Because earlier groups are small in size, security is from natural infrastructure like caves, trees, rocks, stone tools among other innovations like bows and arrows. Traps and tricky gates set to trap or capture wildlife are extended to securing families. The use of ditches and tricky doors or trap doors, tunnels and secret exits evolves to later be built into caves, Egyptian tombs, as well as other empires such as Nubian and Zulu. Needless to say, in most societies dogs are and do befriend man and compliment his security innovations.

Education needs are powered through oral stories, papyrus notes in Egypt and along the Nile, rock paintings across Africa, music and dance, monuments among others offering a capture of dramatic events that are passed from generation to generation. Children learn through apprenticeships and with exception formal religious rituals by shadowing their parents/elders, relatives and experts. Intergenerational and multicultural knowledge powers innovations from calendars to abacci and maps.

Economically there is scarcity of food, water, fire, shelter and medicine (natural) as well as security. To survive, barter trade, an exchange of value in goods and services among individuals, families or communities without cash but rather good for good, good for service, or favors (I owe yous) elves and powers value exchanges for centuries. From salt to stone age tools and later iron tools, leather, furniture, animals and knowledge in the form of a performance, ritual, or icon/ornament. Thus goods and services move from one community to the next without need for cash.

The patriarch/matriarch or head of the household or village alongside the advisors, ambassadors and tradesmen compile regular lists of needs and solutions. Trade routes evolve along land and sea to serve these needs with trade hubs growing into areas of strategic importance economically, culturally and politically. Here taxation not in cash/money but as gold, silver, diamonds or a fraction of the value of the gods crossing the route is introduced and levied to fund security, trade hubs infrastructure as well as support the people within and around the trade hubs.

Transportation and communication becomes critical to this growing network of intra African trade. Along the road, old migration routes evolve into trade routes such as along the Nile, across the Sahara, from the Southern Zulu lands to the Savannah lands as well as Coastal areas of Morocco, Accra, Mombasa and Zanzibar. For many along the coast, water voyage becomes the norm. Boats, canoes and ships power this part of the port and trans atlantic trade. Goods from as far as the Middle East and India are exchanged for gold, minerals and food from inland.

Barter trade does not eliminate conflict or loot and capture from war, raids and attacks but it streamlines knowledge, goods and services exchanges among Africa's people and later the rest of the world. Here beads from fish to clothes from hide, cotton or bark cloth and iron tools, dried or salted food, jewelry, gold, silver, diamonds, ornaments, copper, oils among others are prioritized depending on the needs of the community.

Infact gold, silver, diamonds and other natural resources like land, heads of cattle, goat, sheep, chicken or fish are quantified and used for dowry, taxes, trade or settlements for labor as salaries within monarchs and empires. As societies interact more, settle longer, specialize more and rely on other communities for what they lack, an era of intra Africa trade powered by trade routes , Hubs and ports develops and evolves to sustain the rise and fall of many empires from Zulu in the South to Morocco, Mali and Egypt in the North, Ghana in the West to Ethiopia and Rwenzururu, Buganda in the East.

This intra Africa trade forsters, albeit occasionally interrupted by mercenaries and internal saboteurs/strife and external attacks from other kingdoms. Taxation emerges as a major wealth generator/guarantor for empires and strategic trade hubs, ports or locations are secured as they gain prominence. Tax evasion becomes a punishable offence often by imprisonment, confiscation of wealth or even death. Trade routes become protected by armies as trade becomes critical to the foundation and sustainability of empires and chieftains/settlements. Of particular note are coastal towns like Zanzibar, Cairo Egypt, Accra Ghana among others.

With irrigation, health and cultural innovations having risen out of the first civilizations such as Egypt along the Nile, the Zulu in the South among others (Bantu in the west), security, trade and information (finance, religious, cultural) become critical for later empires. Value is placed on education in math, science and technology. From the abacus in Egypt to Astronomy and medicine by Islamic scholars in Timbuktu, Egypt as well as health, nutrition and architecture alongside christianity in Ethiopia. African empires embrace enlightenment and scholarly exchanges to improve their well being.

Architecture plays a critical role in designing, building, defending education in the cities, capital and people that emerge from the empires. In Egypt and Sudan, pyramids and brick architecture takes root. In

Mali, Timbuktu, libraries and palaces as well as museums take shape while along coastal towns like Mombasa and Zanzibar and Accra, forts for defence, markets for trade and palaces for leadership plus hosting trade ambassadors take form. Defence is mostly through a network of spies, armies (infantry etc) armed with iron tools like bows and arrows, swords, spears and later guns.

Education and libraries lead to advances in record keeping especially for finances and palace histories. Trade and palace advisors are sent to the bes learning institutions within Africa where architects and scholars are invited to develop communities as done in Timbuktu under Mansa Musa. Education too brings more knowledge of astronomy, religion (African, Islam in the North and along the coastal towns and Christianity in Ethiopia), as well as medicine, the arts such as music.

Transportation, another pillar of intra Africa and global trade is powered by both land and sea. The best runners, horses, camels, donkeys, and guards are trained to lead or join trade caravans (group of traders usually representing a community). For sea, boats and ships plus canoes are designed, secured or bought and rowers or sailors trained in the art and science of navigation, combat as well as diplomacy. Along the coast of East Africa Swahili language evolves and becomes the dominant way to conduct trade. Over time Arabs mix with the Bantu people on the East African coast adding new words to the Swahili vocabulary from Arabic.

With their new but shared way of communicating, writing and trading, Swahili spreads across Africa as the language of traders and their guards. Because traders often travel with guards for protection, they bring with them the stigma of Swahili being associated with guards , raids and trouble by the people within the communities they traverse. Swahili remains the most common African language across Africa with potential to facilitate intra Africa Trade.

Noteworthy innovations include writing, languages, weaponry (iron smelting), mining, boat and ship design, architecture for ports and palaces including forts, libraries and museums. Compasses used for navigation are traded or the foundational astronomy, weather and basic science and technology exchanged. Communities that invest in education, security and competitive innovation based on value addition survive longer than those relying on inhouse or old stone age technology.

The development of Zanzibar, Mombasa and other ports or coastal towns do not go ignored by both local and global empires offering critical lessons to the success of Africa pre colonialism and the unlimited potential for Africa and her people. This is the reality beyond the European and Western propaganda and actions that ring in the dark era of colonialism, slave trade and extraction based innovation that strips value from Africa.

The East African ports and coastal towns grow organically mimicking nature and the African way of life. They are not linear, gridlike, pre-planned but rather are a living breathing city that responds to the needs and changes of its citizens. From chiefs to traders, ambassadors, sultans and princes, these ports flourish supporting spice, textile, arms and minerals trade across continents to as far as India and the Oman territories. British plans to later rebuild the city fail throughout the British presence either from a lack of understanding of what makes the people and town thrive or a direct preference to extract as much wealth as possible for the crown before considering any local or urban development commitments leaving architecture plans to be just that, blue prints and delusions of superior designs and plans with little to no context for the peoples culture and needs.

Here language and culture evolves, religion and education exchanges thrive and the ports increase in strategic value often setting off diplomatic and political conflicts or co-opetitions but by far remain in African control or the parties learn to co-exist for the benefit of future trade.

The Indian Ocean and Mediterranian sea see trade grow to the envy of Europe with African chiefs and kings sharing wealth with their communities. Empires like Buganda Kingdom, Ethiopia in the Horn of Africa (North East) among others thrive in this era. Mineral wealth, iron tools, leather, food, hide/leather among other items are exchanged for spices, diplomacy, arms, food, architecture services, textiles plus other items with the world. In Seku Toure's words, "the world needs Africa and Africa does not need the world."

Chapter 6: West – The West's Late Arrival to Developed Shaka Zulus and Haili Selasies

The King of Kings: Ethiopian Emperor Hailie Sellasie. Lion, Protector, Liberator, Educator, Prophet (Source: Public Domain, US Library of Congress).

African military systems incorporated imported and innovative technology but the military edge was usually due to African tactics (Source: Wikimedia).

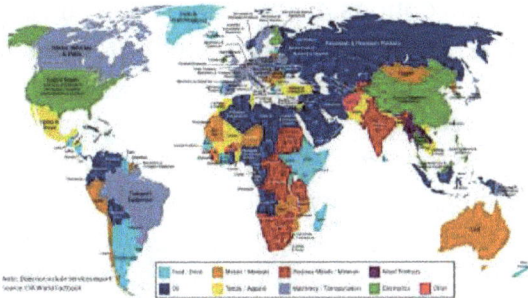

Enlightenment and Economic Development as Propaganda for Uncompensated Wealth Exploitation (Source: CIA World Factbook).

Africa's history and the ways of life of its ancient people are just as critical to todays and tomorrows challenges. Agriculture, raw materials ownership and processing, strategic port and trade links control, and culturally relevant education, people focused democratic leadership and court systems backed by an Africa trained and inspired military are some of the foundational themes and solutions for real effective change and transformation of securing Africa's future. Education brings in the window for financial and literacy and technical innovations complimented by religious, cultural and political exchanges.

Southern Africa boasts of the Zulu nation with Shaka Zulu at the helm while in the North Eastern Horn of Africa Ethiopia thrives under emperor Haile Selassie. Western Africa boasts the Asante kingdom among others with Morocco, Egypt and Mali areas rich in islamic culture, trade routes and enlightenment. As Europe reaches or struggles with its industrial revolution and runs out of sustainable options, there is an increasing need to find alternative sources of wealth, resources and dominance over trade with India and Asia as a whole. Africa increasingly becomes a clear strategic area and of interest especially the Eastern, Western and Southern ports. The Northern/mediterranean and Western Africa ports are closer to Europe and already have some history of relations and trade routes with Europe as early as the Alexandria era and the religious crusades.

Africans for the large part utilise mercenaries, emissaries and other trade ambassadors to do business with the world, often relying on these traders to handle trade route taxes, purchase or barter for needed materials as well as negotiate strategic agreements. The coastal towns increase in political significance as they cater to leaders and diplomats of all sizes from Africa to the Middle East and Asia. The Turkish Oman wars lead to some sultans or their families to seek refuge on the East African coasts emboldening relations between Africa and the Middle East as well as India.

Of the influential trade routes is that between Buganda kingdom and the coastal towns via the savannah plains and ports of Mombasa and Zanzibar play critical roles as strategic outposts. Q'ez Kingdom (Ethiopia and Eritrea) with Queen of Sheba connections mentioned in the Book of Genesis in the Bible shows the earliest relation and influence of African kingdoms as far as the Middle East.

Trade is not the only factor that emboldens African empires. Some like Zulu in the South led by Shaka Zulu and Ethiopia in the East led by Haile

Selassie thrive on African pride and the Ubuntu philosophy. Wealth is controlled by royalty or land communally owned but benefits all with various social political policies in place to serve the local and global needs of their people.

Haile Selassie and other previous rulers of Ethiopia keep the kingdom insulated from global sabotage and coups. They still allow for travel and strategic trade but foreign religion and cultural influence are kept at a distance. This multicultural alignment and affinity albeit among people of different tribes, languages and cultures allow Ethiopia like other empires to stay strong and united under their leadership with a common vision of serving the people. The king/emperor and his emissaries travel around the world, building relationships, exchanging ideas, goods and services and return to Ethiopia to continue the work of educating and empowering the people. There are long periods of stability in Ethiopia with christianity, agriculture, education, a strong military and trade powering the kingdoms rise. Architecture also makes its mark on Ethiopia with the emperor building palaces, schools, libraries, churches or monasteries among other functional buildings.

In the Southern part of Africa, the Zulu nation/kingdom grows and prospers under the mighty and great Shaka Zulu. A warrior, protector and fierce but just leader, Shaka, through military campaigns and annexations expands his empire's reach almost as far North as East Africa due to cultural influence across the Kalahari desert and beyond. He too loves adventures, education and growth but above all treasures his people and land.

Across Africa, the remaining large empires are strong, united and rely on intra Africa as well as trans Atlantic, mediterranean and Indian ocean trade routes. Agriculture, minerals like gold, ornaments, weapons, mercenaries and other services power trade. The relative stability of most towns and cities like Timbuktu in Mali kingdom, Accra in the Gold coast, Limpopo in Zululand and Mombasa or Zanzibar in East Africa allow for the permanent construction of infrastructure like libraries and forts. Effective food storage facilities like grannaries or salt storage units along the coast are secured. And last but not least, palaces are remodeled, designed and adorned with ornaments, crafts, and creative as well as religious or scientific scholars for prestige and human capital development.

On innovation, Arabic takes hold through Islamic instruction to compliment Swahaili on the coasts, Wolof and other thousands of languages bringing with it the math and science discoveries, innovations like levers from Egypt, and values that empower kingdoms and their people alike. Infact Arabic influence along the Eastern and Northern coasts of Africa grows to reach the hinterlands. Mosques, schools and other architecture are built and trade continues to grow such as with Turkish and Ottoman empire in the Middle East.

Chapter 7: South – The Scramble for Empires through Divisions and Inhumane Trade

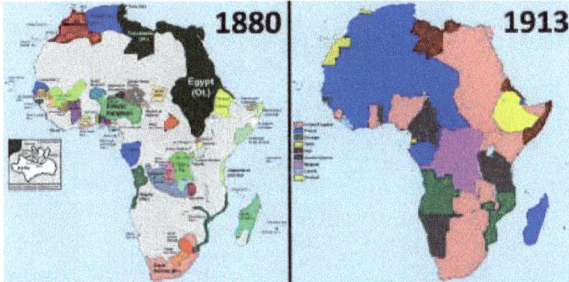

The Scramble for Africa for What the West Lacks. (Source: Map created by davidjl123 / Somebody500 via wikimedia)

National borders, arbitrary by choice, divide communities.
(Source: The Map Archive)

In 1884, Europe, having figured out the sea navigation and "discovered" that the world is bigger and richer than their icy cold lands, decides it wants the rest of the world for itself. With greed and not mutual value based trade as the motive for the ever scarce resources of minerals like gold, copper, diamonds, spices and land for farming food as well factory inputs like cotton or wool, the scramble for Africa and indeed the rest of the world escalates. German chancellor Bismarck invites his neighbor King Leopold of Belgium to host the 1884-85 Berlin Conference with a single perpetual purpose of deciding once and for all how as Europe they would carve up Africa into tiny pieces and take it for themselves with little to no bloodshed amongst themselves while ensuring centuries of wealth extraction and utter robbery of the continents finances, resources and human capital including land and art.

Of the major co-signers to this pact are 'great" Britain, France, Belgium, Germany, Spain, Italy, Portugal, Netherlands among others like Turkey in attendance with the exception of the US which busy with its North American foothold and expansion rejects commitment to imperial presence in Africa. What ensues is a series of propaganda filled with fictional narratives, illusions and justifications mostly deceptive in nature with cross generational implications. "Race" as an idea they have invented serves as a basis for their greed and search for African control justifying their evil actions often in the name of Jesus blessed by the King James Bible or the Pope in Rome. Africa is self servingly "painted as inferior, evil, barbaric, uncivilized" and as told to the European population in need of saving from "Africanism" by the "enlightened European" through indoctrination of false religion, encouragement of self hate and an idolization of all things European against things African or Middle Eastern. This soft-war is meant to culturally, religiously and mentally weaken Africans and create or leverage internal conflict, a divide and conquer strategy and philosophy. Where possible "missionaries, explorers and other colonial experts" commissioned by colonial powers like Britain are sent to spy, infiltrate and report back as well as train African traitors.

Where explorers and missionaries fail in recruiting traitors, coercion and force including assassinations is used. However, for most areas, intermediaries, mercenaries and backing of one kingdom or royal member against the other become the norm for Britain and other "peaceful colonizers." The goal is not assimilation either as the African is "uncivilized". Rather, European values are forced upon communities. Religious and language instruction begins in the relevant romance languages such as English, French, Dutch, German, Spanish, Portuguese among others at the expense of African religion, language and culture.

Not all are patient to test their propaganda. Belgium, Netherlands and Germany do not mince words but deploy force in Central and Southern Africa areas. In the Central African areas, King Leopold puts Africans to work on rubber farms cutting trees for sap. The torture on these plantations is beyond horror, with arms of workers decapitated among other atrocities. Mass graves and genocides happen in the South from Namibia desserts to the Zulu lands with the Boer wars. The resistance of Africans to colonialism is fought on multiple fronts and continues till this day.

With divide and conquer at work, illicit agreements are drafted and signed under European laws to replace laws of the motherland. Britain for example gives monopolistic powers to the British trading companies like the 1660 incorporated and 1672 chartered - Royal African Company in West Africa, involved in the trans Atlantic slave trade; rights to explore, protect, extract wealth and trade on behalf of the Crown under King Charles II, led by his brother the Duke of

York [National Archives, UK GOV]. Queen Elizabeth National Park in Kasese, Uganda among other colonial monuments and stolen land still exist across Africa bearing this historical shame sustained by charity and wildlife conservation efforts from the world's most polluting economies.

Chapter 8: North - The White Man's Burden to Enlighten the Already Wise African

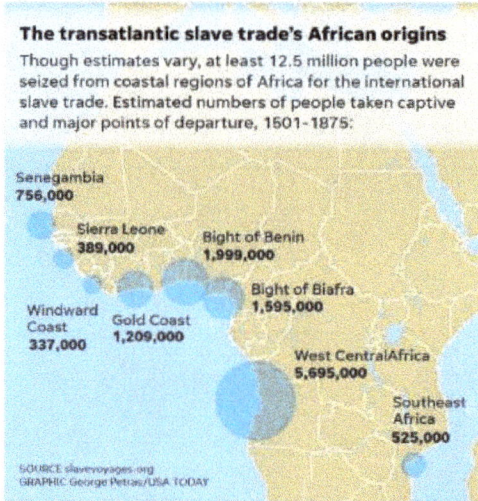

The transatlantic slave trade's African origins

Though estimates vary, at least 12.5 million people were seized from coastal regions of Africa for the international slave trade. Estimated numbers of people taken captive and major points of departure, 1501-1875:

Senegambia
756,000

Sierra Leone
389,000

Bight of Benin
1,999,000

Bight of Biafra
1,595,000

Windward Coast
337,000

Gold Coast
1,209,000

West Central Africa
5,695,000

Southeast Africa
525,000

SOURCE slavevoyages.org
GRAPHIC George Petras/USA TODAY

Slavery, Genocide, Apartheid and Land Theft as used by Rome in ancient Europe becomes an "enlightened" choice of expansionary conquest for European, American and Middle Eastern Imperialism

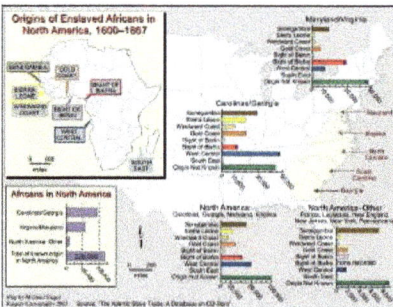

The Atlantic Slave Trade: Slavery lasts 200+ years in the US extended by Jim Crow Laws of Segregation and Mass Incaceration.

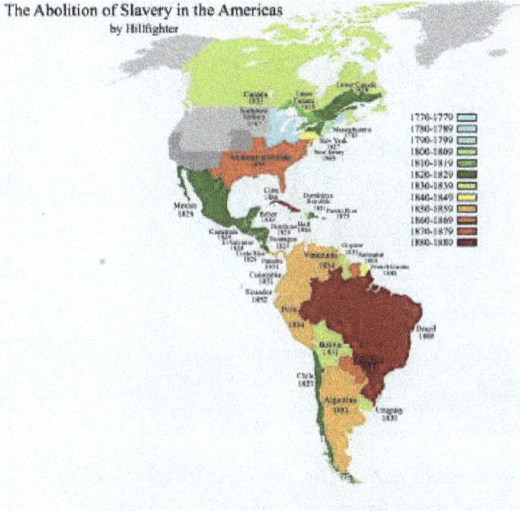

The Abolition of Slavery in the Americas
by Hillfighter

Imperialism, Colonialism and Slavery brought and oppressed Africans globally and resistance to institutionalised oppression through criminal and anti-immigration law continues in Israel, Europe, the Middle East, China and Americas like Brazil and even the UN (no security council seat for AU member state).

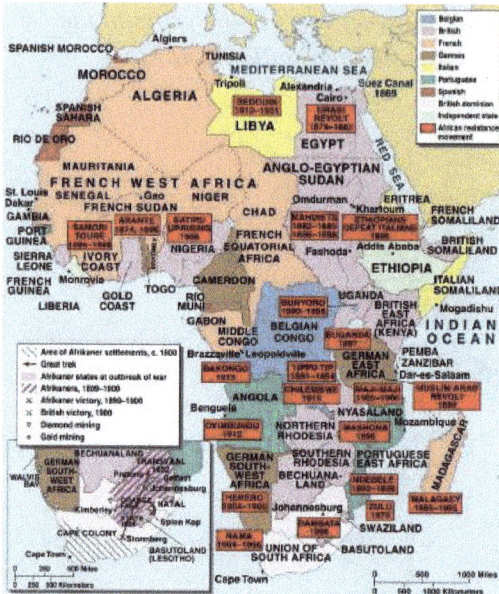

The Arican resistance wars continue to date through Black Consciousness, the African Union and the Global Diaspora (Source: @decolonialatlas).

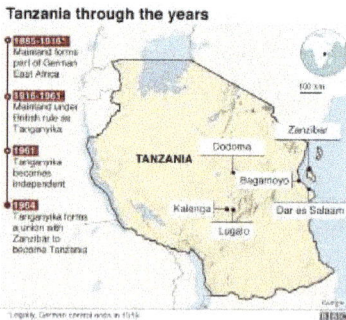

Britain's trickery of Germany during the Treaty of Varseille treaty or the formation of the League of Nations (now the

United Nations) to return the anti colonialist Chiefs skull
(shot by Germans even after he commiteds suicide to avoid
capture like Hannibal from Catharge against Rome) as a
bargaining chip for loyalty to the crown ends on the wrong
side of history (Source: BCC).

Chief Mkwawa's full name:
Born in 1855 and named Ndesalasi, meaning "Troublemaker"
As an adult later named Mtwa Mkwava Mkwavinyika
Mahinya Yilimwiganga Mkali Kuvago Kuvadala Tage
Matenengo Manwiwage Seguniwagula Gumganga, meaning:
"A leader who takes control of the forests, who is aggressive
to men and polite to women, who is unpredictable and
unbeatable, and who has the power that it is only death who
can take him away"
The Germans shortened this to Mkwawa, pronounced
"Mkwava" - but it is now commonly pronounced as it is spelt.
(Source: National Archives, BBC)

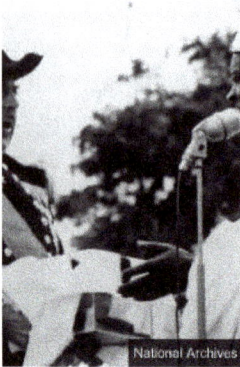

> " I hope too that you and your people will continue to give your unstinted loyalty to Queen Elizabeth II and her heirs and successors"

**Edward Twining,
Tanganyika's British
governor**
As he presented the skull to
Chief Mkwawa's grandson
Chief Adam Saapi in 1954

> " The skull gives us a chance to be proud of people who resisted the colonisers"

Eric Jordan
Mkwawa Museum in Kalenga

The treaty was signed in the Hall of Mirrors in the Palace of Versailles (Source: BBC).

The white man's "burden" to "enlighten" the African should have stayed that, just a thought but as it is an illusion, it still haunts them todate. Africa thrives as Europe struggles to feed and care for her ever growing population with dreams to find the next silk road and be a part of if not control international trade in spices, ammunition, minerals and other raw materials. Tired of European tribalism from fights within European states and empires, all expansionist eyes are on Africa. Africa thrives with empires trading with each other and the world (indians, Arabs, Turks etc) when Europe initiates a centuries old strategy to loot African soil, minerals and bodies including art leaving only evil and darkness in the path. From slave labor to raw materials extraction or export driven agenda, Africa loses its intra Africa agenda and all resources and innovation begins to serve European/western and not African empires and her people.

Ethiopia, Zulu, Morocco among other Kingdoms offer resistance in various ways throughout but the "white man's" enlightenment ultimately leaves a dark chapter in Africa and the world. Priceless art and ornaments, royal wealth, records, weapons as well as strong youth talent are stolen against their will and Africa is robbed naked. Despite "Western"/European propaganda, the African resistance thrives. This resistance is in the form of attacks, rebellions, sabotage, political opposition, decolonizing the mind through art and culture as well as trade and community solidarity. The education of Africans both orally and through visual religion, arts and culture of their history and future keeps the resistance alive from generation to generation.

With colonialism, a pro African, intra Africa development of science and technology reverts to or halts and serves only foreign markets and interests with little to no checks and balances to protect African interests. With free to low cost labor, resources, innovations and wealth, Europe thrives (Amsterdam, Paris, London etc) while Africa is deprived of its growth potential. Those who dare advocate for African interests are banned, censored, exiled, tortured and killed. Rather than "enlighten" Africa, colonialism stunts Africa's progress towards a united, free trade and migration/movement area.

While Zulu kingdom and her people is overpowered after years of counter resistance and other kingdoms are overrun through trickery, deceit, forgery and assassinations or coups, Ethiopia remains standing against Italians and their Pope's blessings of massacres. Italy's future attempts and attacks against Ethiopia prove futile despite their confidence in their "superior weaponry" and their Pope's blessings. Ethiopia's knowledge of its land and culture allow it to stay isolated, making possible surprise attacks and counter attacks. Ethiopia is never colonized and grows to become the beacon of hope, the seed for the pan African liberations as well as anti slave trade movements in Africa, the caribbean and around the world. Due to the disgraceful defeat, Rastafarians, who follow Haile Selassie as their leader are discriminated against by colonial regimes globally who alienate any form of resistance or real African freedom (cultural or economic and political). Like the racist American laws and policies against natural and African hairstyles (afros or cornrows), Rastafarians suffer the same racially biased fate with their cousins in South Africa and the Diaspora where the apartheid regime has hair tests for "race" segregation tests.

Science and technology spurred by intellectual capital across Africa is channeled to extractive empires and regimes who build rails, canals, airports and roads for the sole purpose of speeding wealth extraction from mines, death ridden farms and factories. Cash crops like cotton, tea, coffee, flowers,cocoa among others are prioritized over a balance for African food crops. Sustainable Agricultural practices like inter-cropping are ignored and instead replaced by single crop agriculture leaving soils mineral depleted. New food options replace nutritious traditional food options and only areas like Ethiopia survive this health scourge. From forced labor, low pay to malnutrition and death, the progress of Africa by Africans is frozen under colonial rule due to loss of talent, land and freedom.

PART 3: The Third Eye – Awakening the Sleeping Giant with Two Billion African Voices

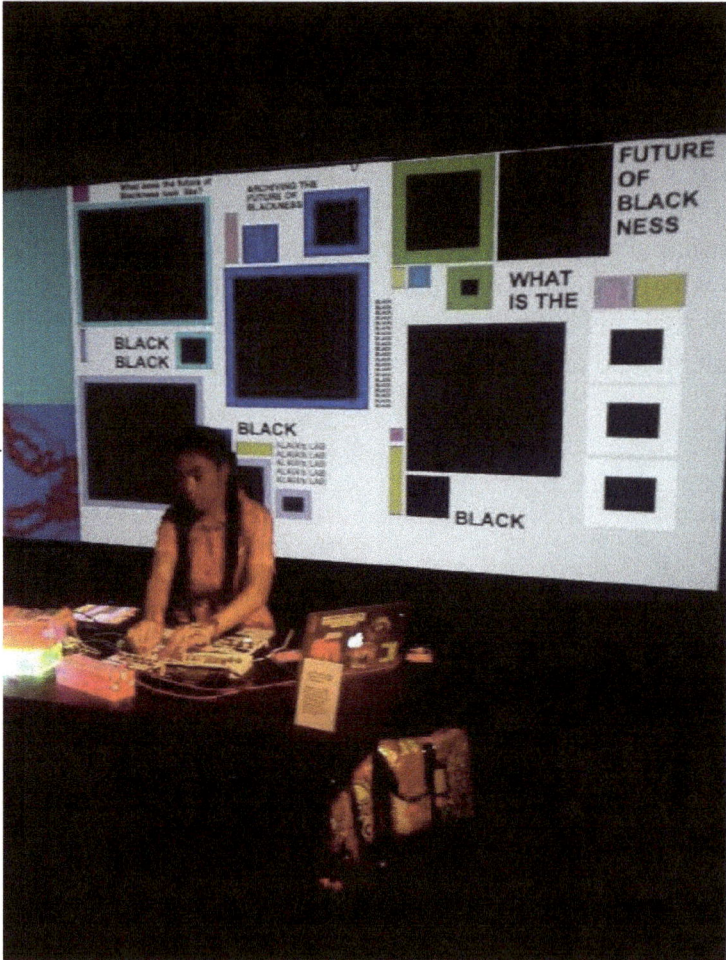

NYU Digital Media Art and Media Student at CultureHub NYC. Photo by Asingia of DreamGalaxy.

Chapter 9: Imagining Freedom – The Beginning of a
Connected Digital Africa

Cell phone and digital broadband connectivity still costly

BrianAsingia.com @brianasingia #AskAsingia

GSMA Mobile Report 2018 (Source: GSMA)

Unlike our parents generation, who were born or even grow up during or towards the end of the greatest lie of all time, "the white man's burden" to enlighten Africa, we have been taught this lie and even seen it fail for a century. Our generation is the bridge that starts the journey to reclaim our true potential by linking our ancestors ways and visions with our children's dreams and realities. We are digital citizens, connected globally through DNA, relationships, experiences and most importantly, a common cause to share a connected and mutually respectful planet as well as galaxy. We are not limited by the lies of the last few centuries but see across the millennia before and the timeless eras ahead of us. We accept our place in this journey as the bridge that must act to secure the future and we embrace this task with humility, respect for our elders and the curiosity and bravery to defend what is rightfully ours and secure our destiny once and for all.

Threads and connections in DNA, language, culture and innovation are rooted in our ancestors ways. From the earlier civilizations to the migration patterns within Africa and across the world, to the global African Diaspora from Europe, Asia to Brazil across Latin America, as a people we are a force destined for unity and influence. From music to Agriculture to mathematics and soon technology and sports, our journey continues but the best is yet to come. From military capabilities to strategic diplomacy and cultural exchanges as a foundation for economic transformation and leverage, the great giant is just awakening. The irony is that the rest of the world has always been aware of the value and potential of Africa, been afraid of it to be precise and embarked on a journey of propaganda and misinformation to devalue and distract this growth: from the invention of the race myth to branding Africa as the dark continent, one in need of aid while its resources are looted from art to minerals and even recreational experiences, Africans having seen the rest of the world for what it is and what it lacks, have come to accept their home and motherland as the everlasting prize, the promised land.

As Africans, in most cases, we are lucky to be taught our history, in school or through stories, and so it is frustrating when one studies abroad only to see a "white washed version of world history" that portrays Africa as a victim, always in need of saving. Such saving includes as verified by public declassified CIA documents assassination of Africa's brightest and strongest men and women, from the losses in apartheid South Africa to the global silence on the genocide in Rwanda initiated by France's arms backing of one tribe against another to the Patrice Lumumba assasination in D.R Congo, and Col Muammar Gaddafi oust in Libya for his vision of a united Africa backed by a gold reserve currency not the colonial era CFA in Western Africa (soon to be replaced by a single West African ECO currency from ECOWAS) among other foreign currencies. True freedom involves ultimate control of security, religion, decision making, education, culture, travel, innovation as well as economic ownership and trade.

To subject oneself to a foreign power in any capacity is but an illusion. All transactions must be handled through strategic negotiations not political photo ops without clear understandings of both short term and long term local and global implications on Africa's security, economy and people. From mineral wealth mines and oil rigs to land ownership and food processing to currency and language adoption and the underlying education, trade and economic policies, Africa needs a reset, because the journey we are on is already compromised. This reset is a two step process that should include a clarification of these weaknesses and the opportunities to address them as well as drafts for Africa owned, controlled and executed 100 year, 50 year and 10 year visions. One to three year visions while ideal are just politicized and can only be subsets or implementations of the above so there is continuity. Leaders can and should only be voted for and supported if they are for and not against Africa explicitly or implicitly. The era of just getting by while the rest of the world innovates, expands its influence and extracts Africa's wealth must stop now.

Visions with no action are nothing and as such, Africa must be aware of the reasons for failure in the past for they are bound to still without explicit political will as history does repeat itself or at least follow a systematic pattern. From internal sabotage to foreign meddling and influence both diplomatic (cultural, religious or education) and direct (militarily or economic sanctions) one must find ways like China, Cuba and Russia have to march forward at all costs, understanding that giving in to the enemy of progress is treason and failure of our duty to our ancestors, ourselves and our children. The internet and technology can play a critical role in helping us remember our past, work to improve our present and celebrate the future we create. Technology through media, travel, music, film, education, and trade has made us aware of each other more than ever as a global Diaspora and a people. Let us leverage this shared knowledge and history to make the next century and millennium a future we deserve. It starts with a commitment to be part of the solution and not the problem, to do our own part in our own way to advance the cause, and most of all, to be vigilant and aware of the enemy in our path and within our communities.

It takes a village to police ourselves, support each other and create the future we want.

No man is an island. Individual rights are nothing without a community. Individuals make a society and as such, whether we like it or not we each have a role to play in this movement and we can either support or hurt our chances of success. There is power and strength in unity, so before agreeing to what the future we want looks like, that is the one place we can start. Our local communities, our cultures, languages and histories layered on technology to inspire innovative solutions for the next century are all we need to get started. It is the first step that is difficult, the understanding of the mission and committing to the vision. We can each in our own ways find ways to contribute, ones that enhance and do not hurt the cause.

Half a century after African leaders bring most of their people to independence, the African globally is just awakening from the mental, spiritual, physical, social and economic shackles of colonialism. The sleeping giant, Africa, is "no longer at ease". Separated across generations by and over arbitrary borders, leadership assassinations, and racial segregations as is in South Africa and some Northern/Arabic areas, Africans of all walks and cultures are awakening to their ancestral connections. This is all thanks to the mobile phones, both smart and feature phones.

Cell phones, introduced as communication tools with foreign brands like Nokia, Samsung among others run on foreign owned networks and ex-apartheid firms like MTN that often operate as regional monopolies just as power, energy, oil, construction, mining and other foreign owned service offering firms are. Despite this lack of local or majority African ownership and as a result lack of adequate and effective taxation and local meaningful job creation and reinvestment, Africans are now digitally connected towards a solutions design, implementation and scaling society.

Facebook, Whatsapp, Twitter, Google and sites like Wikipedia, Youtube, Amazon or Microsoft, the digital sphere bring Africans closer where their leaders still bribed by colonial spoils have failed them. For example, France, rather than willingly exit Africa "negotiated"/imposed a "Continuation of Colonialism" or colonial tax, among which is the CFA (a common West African currency) printed in France. In addition, the French Finance Ministry has rights to hold, invest and use without sharing the investment returns up to 80% of the West African reserves as they please, a ridiculous economic price to pay for attachment to colonial wealth extractors. Other terms are colonial debt for the benefits of colonialism, automatic confiscation of national reserves, right of first refusal on any raw or natural resource discovered in the country, priority to French interests and companies in public procurement and public spending, exclusive right to supply military equipment and train the country's military officers, right for france to pre-deploy troops and intervene military in the country to defend its interests, obligation to make French the official language of the country and the language for education, obligation to use France colonial money FCFA (about $500 Billion USD), obligation to send France annual balance and reserve report, renunciation to enter into military alliance with any other country unless authorized by France, and obligation to ally with France in situation of war or global crisis [Bloomberg]. Independence in West Africa and indeed most of Africa is still an illusion, defended by pro colonial experts and middle men benefiting from the status quo. The digital connectedness allows Africans to see evil for what it is; from declassified CIA records of African leaders assassinations such as that of patrice Lumumba to France's interference in Algeria's democratic and economic transformation demands for regime change, a sabotage that has held the North African state years behind its Moroccan and North African neighbors [VOA].

It is technology and in particular mobile with social media albeit with western influence and bias that has led to the overthrow of leaders like Col. Muammar Gaddafi (a pan African visionary with political and economic independence ideas like single currency for Africa backed by gold) only to be replaced with a pseudo failed state and soon to be military regime financed by Saudi Arabia with a US silent approval [WSJ Article]. As a contrast, other leaders toppled or who resign due to youth and women led grassroots efforts include Tunisia's Zine El Abidine Ben Ali, Egypt's Hosni Mubarak, Sudan's Omar Al-Bashir, Algeria's President Abdelaziz Bouteflika, Zimbabwe's Robert Mugabe, South Africa's Jacob Zuma among others. For most of these nations including Zimbabwe, social media is taboo, often shut off by lifetime/perpetual regimes like Uganda's Yoweri Kaguta Museveni to limit people's voices (Uganda even has a social media tax, a sign of the genius behind Ugandan policy makers who prioritize taxing people's lives and survival over multinational corporations).

Politics aside, mobile technology in Africa provides a window into what it means for an African imagined freedom as our ancestors Kwame Nkrumah, Patrice Lumumba, Nelson Mandela, Muammar Gaddafi, Sako Toure, Julius Nyerere and Kenneth Kaunda among others would have wanted. In picking up the baton where they left after half a century of assassinations of African leaders by western powers, sabotage, media propaganda and daylight robbery of art, minerals and illicit fund transfers, Africans young and old, home and foreign are educated at using technology to research, learn, share, organize and make real transformation in Africa a possibility.

The "future African phone" and mostly smartphones including connected devices like the internet of things (IoTs) is now the identity, bank, school, television, computer, laboratory, hospital and timeless technology of "**The Last Digital Frontier**". With the average African having two or more phones and no computers, Africa is a mobile first and perhaps mobile or connected device only frontier. Africa's past, present and future is intertwined with a connected digital Africa and globe.

Chapter 10: Quantum Generational Leaps – Leapfrogging
Western Industrial Revolutions

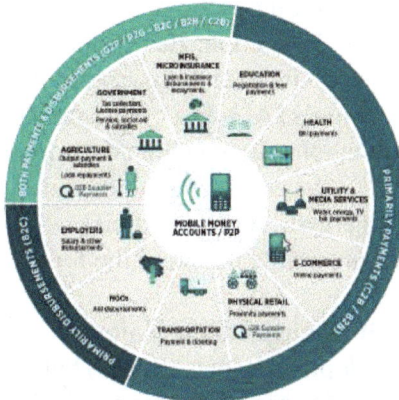

*Fintech in Africa: Africa is Second to China in Mobile Money
Adoption (Source: GSMA).*

*Sample Lendable Innovation Fintech Ecosystem (Source:
Lendable).*

The narrative of leapfrogging western revolutions is neither true nor false, but it is certainly premature. As mentioned by Thion Niang of Akon Lighting Africa at the Africa Rising event in 2018 at Brookings, DC; Africa has to fix the basics such as Agriculture, Education, Health and Energy before we can dream and claim even bigger seats at the table. Indeed the African Union's (AU) Big Four agenda focuses on the same logic with emphasis on youth and women employment. Ark Invest CEO, Catherine Wood, notes that DNA Sequencing, Robotics, Energy Storage, Artificial intelligence (A.I) and Blockchain are the pillars of the fourth industrial revolution.

The AU's Agenda 2030 aligns with the United Nations (UN) Sustainable Development Goals (SDGs) but as the World Bank and UN are yet to successfully economically transform an African sector or area, there is a need for a women and youth driven Africa first agenda. Leapfrogging as a term is misplaced since most of the technologies imported and tried fail due to "technology transfer challenges" as well as limitations of capacity and government or private sector to scale service delivery to the people. In particular, centralized systems like oil, gas and hydro power generation do not scale easily to rural areas. Thus related technologies like landlines, or even now mobile, computers, connected devices like cars, flights and rails that would rely on fibre optic cables along power lines or underground and decentralized wifi spots for connectivity are capped. Transportation links of roads and railways are also not as accessible due to "extraction based design" of infrastructure. Reads and rails in colonial times times are from resource areas to the ports at sea or airports as opposed to also linking for internal intra Africa trade limited by militarized and bureaucratic borders with insane tariffs.

It is again the mobile phone that has broken this isolation and siloed ecosystem when diplomacy, politics, policy and legislation has failed. Phones can hold power 12-24 hours a day allowing trade, banking, texting, calling, browsing and e-commerce across borders and cultures. One such innovation is mobile money with M-PESA in Kenya leading the innovation curve processing billions of dollars across regions and continents with the Global Diaspora. Jumia, Flutterwave, Paystack, Uber, AirBnB are all other foreign owned or registered mobile innovations based in or operating in Africa. Mall for Africa and its recent partnership with DHL, a global shipping business is an example of joint ventures, mergers and local adaptations needed for effective and inclusive access and scale across Africa [TechCrunch].

Identity and in particular digital identity is at the core of Africa's challenges followed by a data strategy as well as a strategic 10-100 year digital service delivery roadmap. For "values based innovations" to succeed, Africa starts with the greatest challenges of all time, digitizing two billion identities. Thankfully, India, China, Estonia are places to learn from with the US and EU approaching digital identities and privacy differently especially Estonia with its e-estonia digital citizenship as the minimum service delivery requirement. This allows for faster, safer, and secure linkage to the multiple identities or characteristics, roles and personas. Africans need to navigate and lead the fourth industrial/digital revolution. Current paper based systems generate 80% waste and 80% cost savings can be realized outright in digitizing service delivery. Kenya, Rwanda, South Africa and some parts of the Nigeria government services among other countries are already showing progress with the African Union leading the charge. Such complimentary AU initiatives are the Single Africa Passport ideally electronic longterm to integrate with digital ecosystems, Single Air Transport, and Single Continental Africa Free Trade Area (AfCFTA) for borderless trade and movement of human capital and finance.

With digital IDs resolved, data is better mapped, shared and analyzed among interdependent systems to deliver self service or guided but transparent government and private/social service effectively at scale. Data on blockchain can bring transparency to budgeting, policy, service delivery, trade and finance. Critical areas like resource mining, land reallocation/ownership title deeds, banking, savings, insurance, investments and agriculture are all powered on the Blockchain for transparency and trust. The satellite internet efforts in Rwanda, data fibre cables by Facebook, Google Fi, Zimbabwean billionaire's LiquidNet (an EcoNet subsidiary) for connectivity, data and wifi as well as other cloud data infrastructure are the foundation on which "The Last Digital Frontier" success relies. With data at 5G speeds comes an Africa ready for global trade and influence.

Chapter 11: Behind Virtual Curtains – A Young Africa
Emerges to Create its Future

Afrian Union Agenda 2063 Seven Core Pillars (Source: AU.int).

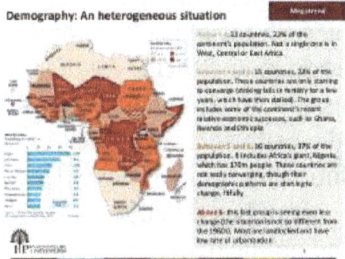

An Emerging Youth Demands a Seat at the Table.

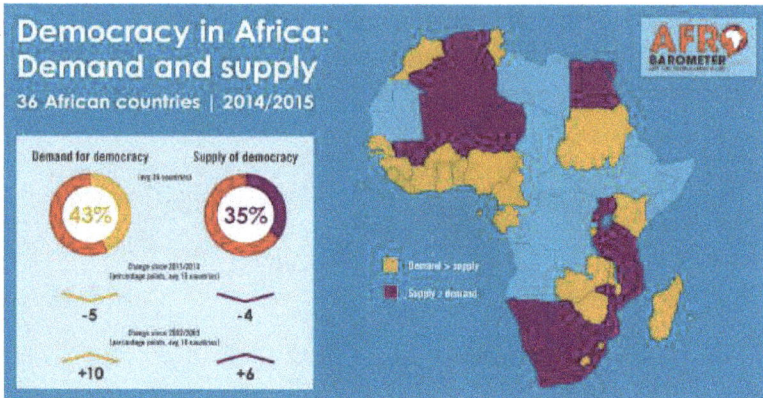

Populations in Countries like Uganda must embrace #PeoplePower to move the needle towards real growth (Source: Afrobarometer Data Report).

By 2030, Africa has the world's largest youth demographic with 50% under thirty years old. These youth bring down dictatorships, demand change, transparency and accountability. In Southern Africa, with racial and economic tensions brought forth or sustained from apartheid, youth demand the attention of politicians and government to serve them not just a few with apartheid wealth and influence. Indeed across Africa where revolutionary regimes have been toppled, the anti-suppression movement has failed to make a dent in realizing the "economic and political" freedom the fighters imagined due to foreign intervention or lack of sufficient support for African values and expectations (return of land, art, ownership, rule of law, livable wages, education, trade among others). Some regimes refuse to draft succession plans or pass the baton to the youth clinging to power like a dying lice, refusing to fall off its host. As per Mo Ibrahim, some African leaders can barely stand up or walk but continue to extend term limits or remove them entirely embracing a timelessness beyond even Egyptian pharaohs who believed they were gods but mostly in the afterlife.

This failure by leadership to have long term vision in 3, 10, 50 and 100 year road maps and plans allows for politicized goal shifting and propaganda without action to be normalized and accountability ignored. For most of the youth, their lives are a lie; educated with a promise of jobs only to graduate into a 30-60% unemployment line in areas like Nigeria in West, Uganda in East, DR Congo in Central and South Africa in Southern Africa. The dangerous see voyages North towards Europe and America for dreams that don't exist, often retracing steps of their ancestors taken against their will in chains is filled with underground slave markets in Mali and Libya as well as loss of life in the sea/oceans, a humble reminder of how the undying old guard eating the scraps of colonial robbers have failed the youth.

With cabinets that barely understand the complex and critical legal, technology and security challenges of today, foreign consultants and not African or Diaspora youth and experts are contracted to design, implement, secure and operate both physical and digital infrastructure continuing the colonial goal of prioritizing foreign talent and values with the obvious revenue, taxation, and data/security/intelligence benefits lost. This cycle of untapped human capital shamelessly starts with African leadership.

Neglected at home and segregated against abroad, the African youth caught between unemployment and drowning in the sea are no longer waiting for change but are creating and living the change they wish to see (#theAfricaWeWant), a "DreamAfrica". From entrepreneurship to small and medium sized businesses (SMEs), youth are leading integration of science and technology in designing their own Africa focused solutions with global scale potential. Unfortunately for most, the legal, intellectual property (IP) and policy (business, trade and investment) frameworks are stuck in the extractive (colonial era) not the intra Africa plus global trade periods.

The AU with its signed, ratified and now effective Africa Continental Free Trade Area (AfCFTA) seeks to address this allowing for a common market across Africa for goods and services backed by a free movement of people. This is all not good news to colonial loyalists and traitors who view their current commissions on exclusive but limited trade deals with non transparent or mutually beneficial experts sufficient. They fail to grasp the urgency of a value addition chain/process across Africa as demonstrated by Ethiopia, Rwanda, Senegal and even Morocco whose AU interest has been less than consistent in pushing for regional trade within Africa with an eye for global competitiveness. Wifi in Rwanda Air, satellite connectivity pilots, solar farms by Morrocco for energy and Ethiopia's industrial and waste treatment and rail initiatives are just a few examples of African and not just national thinking.

The youth navigate the AU agenda with minimal wait time for old regimes, leveraging technology instead to deliver on identity, data, service and security. This is being achieved through online support communities like Silicon Africa on Facebook, TEFConnect.com for Tony Elumelu Entrepreneurs and Whatsapp or Twitter for business and networking. New VOIP/internet calling and communications platforms are being innovated out of Nigeria and Virtual Private Networks (VPNs) used to work around government censorship of youth and activist voices. Africa's neglected and underutilized resource are its youth human capital. Leaders are aware of this ticking time bomb that is unstoppable yet their ego and political greed is prioritized over the dream and future of an entire continent.

Chapter 12: Our Original Story – The Reclaiming of Africa's History and Art by Africans

Africa Regional Intellectual Property Office (ARIPO) is separate from other regional IP offices with minimal consistency in IP enforcement across Africa.

As our ancestors taught us, everyone has a story. From society origin stories to folklore and later stories of resistance and liberation movements, youth are realizing the anti-Africa, anti-black propaganda from the west and within Africa and reclaiming their narratives. Through ecosystem research and creative initiatives, talented youth both foreign and African educated are connected via technology (online and offline) to design, create and own Africa focused solutions with global competitiveness. Finance through Fintech, media via studios like Nollywood and streaming platforms like DreamGalaxy TV, iRokoTV and AllAfrica.com as well as health, transport and energy via innovations like MallforAfrica and Akon Lighting Africa are being disrupted by Africa focused solutions with intra Africa and global scalability.

The old colonial narrative of Africa as the dark continent is checked by social media campaigns like #TheAfricaTheyNewerShowYou and #TheAfricaWeWant reports as well as #TheLastDigitalFrontier reports and features. For youth, media, arts, travel, business, trade and innovation powered by education through mobile technology whether its music concerts, videos, films, animations, documentaries, live streams or events offers the perfect window to own, create and share their African stories and narratives. Journalists, authors and creatives are leading the way where politicians have failed to provide an inspiring vision of Africa [Binyavanga Wainaina, How to Write About Africa].

Data too plays a critical role but years of colonial pencil pushing across Africa, lack of reliable power and a bureaucracy from the 20th century make data acquisition, reliability and analysis as well as long term retention for innovation a challenge. This does not stop Open Data initiatives like Opendataafrica.org, Gov Zero pilots alongside government pilots to track, collect and visualize data. Even the African Development Bank (AfDB) with it's data.afdb.org compliments the efforts as should all governments including the African Union reports and operations. Others are Afrobarameter.org for surveys as well ARIPO.org for African intellectual property data.

While arts and creatives are leading this movement through art, film and music, science and technology innovations lag behind foreign innovations or techtransfer. Payments, banking, and transfers out of Africa are near impossible for large amounts or refunds as are a lack of a single pan African payments platform.

This proliferation of siloed and isolated regional innovations is made worse by regional telecom monopolies and fragmented finance policy among governments. Regional cloud hosting zones are almost non existent with Amazon, Microsoft and LiquidNet pushing to change this amidst fragmented to non existent/enforceable privacy and IP policies.

Despite youth creativity and enthusiasm, leaders lack the will to support their youth against foreign subsidiaries in areas of financial, legal, IP, privacy and cyber security compliance. It is easier for a US or EU registered company to serve Africans and the global diaspora at scale than an African registered firm due to African bureaucracy, paper pushing and a lack of transparency and consistency on legal and security compliance. Here the African Union does not move fast enough to prioritize human capital development and implement effective seamless intra Africa trade. IP, legal, security and tax requirements for African women and youth to trade or work within Africa while competing with global companies and their tax exempt subsidiaries becomes an unfair ecosystem with an illusion of globalization that benefits one side against the other. African Stock Exchanges too lack the leverage and brand history to attract more local listings and the Jumia (a German registered e-commerce player in Africa) listing at The New York Stock Exchange (NYSE) with a controversial branding as an "African Company" is an example of the bias towards foreign registered firms in financing, ease of trade and capital transfer who continue to outcompete African or Diaspora owned firms and capture market share plus revenues without critical local wealth creation on the continent through stock ownership,meaningful human capital development, and ultimately effective taxation and intra African reinvestment from scale. African Exchanges must combine to increase deal flow, capitalization and trade volume as well as brand identity.

Politics and in particular legal and policy enforcement are also increasingly driven by youth and women. Ethiopia women leaders, Rwanda's leadership, South Africa's 50% women cabinet and the AU youth focused agenda are wonderful examples. Politicians can no longer ignore the lack of correcting our history as Senegal does with its Black culture museum among other countries like Nigeria demanding the return of African art and wealth generating monuments in Western museums. This should be a non negotiable prerequisite for the right pro Africa trading partners who acknowledge their wrongs and embrace a new era of mutual respect in global trade. To make matters worse, art and culture as well IP theft and appropriation continues with meaningful work by ARIPO and other intra Africa IP efforts stifled by limited enforcement. African youth research ends up registered as foreign IP even when the work was created in Africa by Africans or alongside guest scholars/fellows or exchange programs.

PART 4: The Fourth Revolution – Creating Africa's Promised Future of Infinite Opportunity

An automated population map from Facebook Research Team using A.I

Western Media and IT Firms are Digitizing Africa with Little to No African Engagement or AU Data Policies and Regulations to Protect Critical Data

BrianAsingia.com @brianasingia #AskAsingia

Chapter 13: Pan Africanism - #Africapitalism for the Real "Wakanda" in the 21st Century

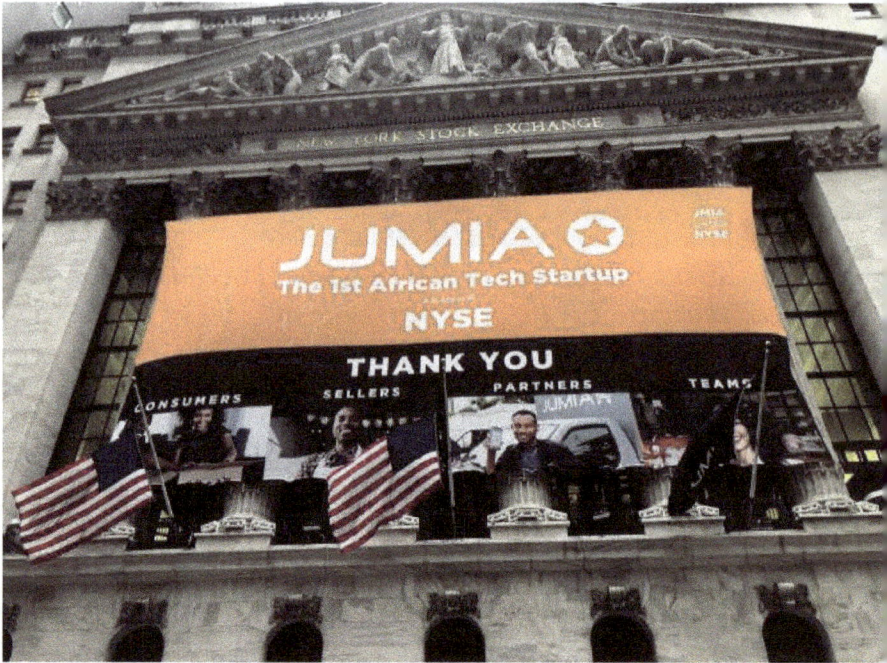

April 2019 IPO Market Listing by Jumia. (Source: NYSE)

Jumia NYSE Listing in Q1 2019: African company? (Source: SEC site mobile screenshot by Asingia)

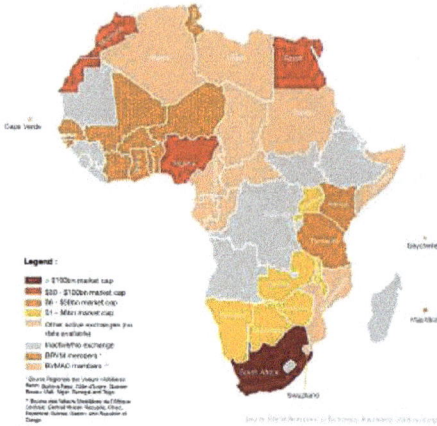

Overview of African stock exchanges at 29 December 2017

African Exchanges need Regional Consolidation and Cross Listing Support for Increasing Capitalisation and Volume (Source: World Federation of Exchanges, Bloomberg, Stock Exchanges in Africa)

Ugandan MPs mandating government ownership of assets and subsidizing "investor" contracts without a clear understanding of corporate legal strategies and share dilution is one way Africa continues to lose its wealth with politicians claiming credit for change when in reality they are responsible for the loss of value. The Tullow Oil stalled oil drilling and underutilized capacity of Uganda oil discovery murred in corruption and license transfers is another example of egocentric political priorities derailing genuine job creation opportunities in a nation with high unemployment.

Mr Tony Elumelu, Nigerian Billionaire and philanthropist is training the next generation of African innovators through TEFConnect.org and his colleague Aliko Dangote of Dangote Enterprises which includes cement, food growing and processing as well as Oil refining are inspiring the next African millionaires and billionaires. The youth have African role models invested in them who care deeply about the continent unlike the majority of foreign wealth or corruption ridden illicit financial flows ($50 Billion annually) out of Africa per year. This Africapitalism is stifled by wannabe investors wasting months or years in due diligence for $10,000 to $50,000 deals due to lack of data, financial literacy, local knowledge, investor readiness and a long term investment culture including access to capital markets by both Africans and the global diaspora. While SMEs are the heart of African economies, investors need to focus on industry due diligence with a global mindset. Starting with $100,000 or above minimal seed rounds will not lead to an African IPO or successful exit overnight and as such real longterm investors are needed on the continent and from the global Diaspora as well as local pensions to support creative, science and technology (STEAM) innovations.

The AfDB, Ghana, Rwanda among other entities are all looking at infrastructure and in particular real estate such as innovation Hubs (coworking spaces) which fall short by relying on existing power structures (oil, gas, hydro) frequented by power cuts and load shedding rather than complementing these projects and the national power grids with centralized solar power farms like Morocco has or decentralized offgrid solutions like MKopa and solar by Akon Lighting Africa. In trying to replicate Silicon Valley, African leaders and their foreign experts are forgetting the role of culture and values in design and innovation. The survivor/hustle mentality, peer to peer sharing/network models, decentralized access as well as iterative innovation need not be imported for they already exist alongside the African culture of connectivity driven by community empowerment values like Ubuntu within the motherland. What's lacking is the political will to enforce laws and protect home grown innovations and assets including natural assets like land, food and human capital.

Investments in infrastructure should be strategic to support youth and women efforts locally complimented by local as well as global networks of experts, markets and capital. Digital identities, service delivery like banking, taxation or waivers for early local companies, and education should be a priority with a stronger foundation of food, energy, transport, connectivity, health and security (both physical and digital).

Africapitalism is the economic philosophy that the African private sector has the power to transform the continent through long-term investments, creating both economic prosperity and social wealth according to African billionaire Mr. Tony Elumelu of the Tony Elumelu Foundation [Africapitalism: A Management Idea for Business in Africa? by Kenneth Amaeshi]. South Africa is decades behind due to its unresolved land and economic inclusion challenges with over 70% of the land owned by 10% of the mostly white population, a mistake and dark shadow of the apartheid regime. Areas like DR. Congo, Algeria, Tunisia, Libya, Cameroon, Sudan and Mali while making waves towards democracy (not that western democracy or western backed democracy is by itself the solution to inclusive economic growth) are at risk of sliding back if the AU does not provide consistent support for human dignity and human capital development.

Globally backed corruption of over $50 Billion in annual illicit financial flows from Africa with the help of foreign and local banks, lawyers and governments is one of the major sources of savings and capital for food, education, health, legal and security needs. Pension funds, $300 Billion in value can also return twice (2X) their current foreign investments return on investment (ROI) if invested home on the continent of Africa. The $160 Billion in sovereign wealth funds complimenting Foreign Direct Investment (FDI) such as Morocco's solar farms and Ethiopia's rail, air and manufacturing investments are models worth emulating and replicating. The era of seeking solutions only out of Africa should slowly come to an end if expenses like conferences, training and awards abroad or even sports are instead hosted on the continent as Ethiopia (Addis Ababa) is for Davos 2020.

Charity begins at home and hospitality is indeed an African value. With a return of all looted art and ornaments, implementation of really independent institutions unlike the CFA (colonial tied projects), land rights as basis for economic ownership for business as well as IP enforcement to reflect the needs, demands, and dreams of our ancestors, youth and women innovators will deliver a strong foundation for #TheAfricaWeWant and the success of AU's #Agenda2063. Africapitalism means a united africa with regional implementation, an intra Africa trade and pro Africa creative, medical, Agricultural, mining, legal and tech solutions ecosystem.

Chapter 14: Own Your Story – Media and the Rise in IP Ownership by Africans

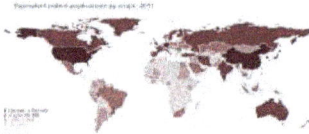

Africa needs aggressive IP protection. (Source: World IP Report 2018)

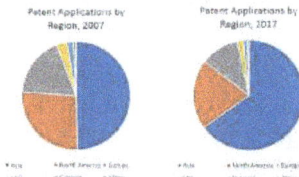

Recent Asian (Chinese) IP Filings are the Highest Globally

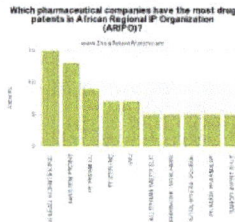

(Source: WIPO ReportFrontier
Health, Security, Electronics and Food Industries need Innovation Protection from Global Monopolies.

       Identity (physical and digital identities), Ownership (creative, economic, political and cultural), Trust and Scale (Global Africapitalism not Nationalism) i.e IoTs are the pillars of **The Last Digital Frontier**. Owning our African stories (personal, family, career, political, cultural, financial) is the first step to establishing who we are, where we come from and where we want to go. This is a village effort and everyone's responsibility to contribute anyway they can from the 1.3 Billion Africans on the motherland to the 250 Million and growing in the global diaspora. Africa is more than Nollywood, Kwaito, Afrobeats and safaris. #TheAfricaTheyNeverShowYou is the beginning of how we should hold our ancestry, progress and future to higher standards like the royalty we are.

Digital innovation has been measured by a colonial thinking mistake of foreign acquisitions and licensing instead of home grown scale and global influence through foreign affiliates powered by the Global Diaspora. Progress starts with creative, economic and political ownership of both creative and digital innovations. This includes design, research, prototypes and products or services. The production pipeline value addition such as for electronics, medicine, food and culture should be strategic security priorities. With raw materials from copper, cobalt, oil, gold, and food as well as human capital to develop the materials, more youth and women need to be trained, funded and supported to own, operate and scale more of this value chain. Made in Africa should be prioritized to mean more than mere product parts assembly or just foreign firms with subsidiaries in Africa for the purpose of extracting raw materials with little value add.

Gradual transitions need to be made from importing to assembling and ultimately component making so that Africa becomes the global leader in digital and electronic components sourcing. Why export raw materials only to pay 3X or more for imports of complete cell phones, IoT devices, cars, refrigerators among other critical products and services?

The importance of African's owning more including their narrative can start with the perception around land ownership, title deeds policy and collateral culture. The thief of Africa's wealth is clear and apologetic tones need not be made for a clear historic wrong. The land must be cleared for a DreamAfrica where Africans feel at home. Here legal policies to protect ownership from land to creative IP as well as science and technology innovations need fast updates and global enforcement. A single Africa IP initiative is overdue.

The narrative youth demand and are indeed creating is that of job creation, ownership, economic and legal support across Africa and globally backed by reliable digital connectivity. This is not the case for Cameroon, now under a civil war with French owned pseudo monopolies in Agriculture (bananas) in cahoots with the government at the expense of people's loss of land, health and ultimately lives and family for many close to the ever expanding plantations. Like the World Bank trade and investment policies disasters in Jamaica, bribery for loans in South Africa among others, the spin here is that these plantations create jobs (in exchange for your land, health from pesticides, life from illness or conflict and gradually loss of local food production capacity). Extraction based policies of the colonial era should be seen for what they are and resisted at all cost from the grassroots to the African Union and its global allies including the Diaspora.

It is also exciting that youth are leveraging technology for challenging politicians and demanding change. Care should also be taken here in the mass hysteria social media and automation era with media blackouts, censorships or targeted biased campaigns/propaganda. Such campaigns can also be foreign initiated, supported or influenced/hijacked and as such the core goals and values should never be forgotten for any revolution or movement. Qadaffi, Sadam, the ICC targeting African leaders are just a few examples in a clear contrast to the UN and indeed the world not acting in issues of DR Congo, Rwandan genocide and apartheid in

South Africa to name a few. Rwanda spent twelve million US dollars to resolve genocide cases in local community courts while the ICC spent more than a billion to process only fifteen cases according to Rwandan president H.E Paul Kagame.

The recent win by Ethiopia against "Dutch" teams for the IP rights to Njera, is just an example of the danger of foreign resource theft, cultural design and art appropriation with ultimate ownership as the goal through shady legal schemes. Here technology can and should be leveraged to bring transparency and value addition partnerships in industries like mining, manufacturing, scientific research, medical testing, art and culture, sports, Agriculture, Fashion among others. Hiring local and Diaspora engagement and contracting with the right legal protection is the right start but not the end.

Chapter 15: DreamAfrica Digital – AI, Cybersecurity, and Blockchain in Africa (IoTs)

Akoin: Africa's first digital currency has the potential to engage the continent and global Diaspora (Source: Akoin.org)

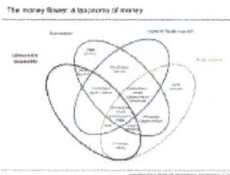

Digital Identities, Ownership, Trust and Scale (IoTs) are critical to public private partnerships and service delivery.

Jack Ma, founder of Alibaba while speaking on Digitizing Emerging Markets at the World Economic Forum 2019 shares his EEEETTTT (Education Entrepreneurship e-frastructure e-government for Trade, Training, Tourism and Technology) Hub platform in partnership with Rwanda where Rwanda businesses like coffee farmers with transactions under $1 million sell tax free to chinese consumers through a mobile digital platform. While China is pushing its Belt and

Road Initiative (the New Silk Road), Africa needs to take care of its economic foundation (food, education, health, energy, single digital identity) through a digital transformation. The new platforms mostly cloud based and soon relying on edge based artificial intelligence (A.I) and service delivery (including robotics) will be powered by blockchain and cybersecurity automation for an intra Africa Digital Free Trade Zone with global competitiveness.

A.I in particular has a lot to offer the continent from powering education via localization and dynamic content delivery, health via progressive data driven research and service delivery with higher relevance, Agriculture for both IoT driven farming with sensor technology and vertical farms with precise nutrient delivery. Finance, census, budgeting, trade, taxation, elections and in fact all service delivery both public and private could benefit from a data driven, self service and automated process both for scalability and reliability.

Recent youth innovations in A.I are malaria detecting programs with minimal blood tests, sign language to audio/speech translators, African language localization and mobile money transfers and banking, credit or health care service delivery among other use cases. A.I in Africa as with most technologies is still limited by a western values design limitation and default support of African languages, cultures and expectations is slim to none. Privacy concerns for example from companies like Facebook in emerging markets are left un addressed as are UNICODE support for local languages like the thousands of African languages. Even where support is provided, it is not the default or local communities are used to western languages as is the case for Ethiopians use of English over Amharic both at home as well as in the global Diaspora [Zaugg, Isabell]. Dynamic language detection and translation can be powered by A.I as is in Google's Android Q update of fall 2019 to support intra Africa trade, education and cultural exchange digitally across borders and cultures with languages like Swahili.

Automated Cybersecurity addresses the core issue of digital identities or lack thereof in **The Last Digital Frontier.** With the AU approving but yet to implement single African passports for all Africans and e-governance still in early stages for both public and private institutions, service delivery is delayed by bureaucracy (including bribes and manual paper work) and limited to slow identification methods. Biometric identity solutions being piloted by the likes of Dangote Foundation and the Bill and Melinda Gates Foundation in separate projects as well as digital passports could play a role in digital identity solutions that increase the effectiveness of data driven and automated self service delivery while lowering the operational cost.

In **The Last Digital Frontier** (Africa), a common or coordinated privacy policy is non existent threatening the potential for trillion dollar e-commerce, digital banking, communications, health and e-insurance economies. Indeed cross border trade logistics, port logistics for both operations and import export, taxation as well as financial investments or payments (mobile or wire transfers) require complex complex encryption and transparency for audit and trust purposes. With A.I, pattern recognition and automated cyber threat detection, cybersecurity plans can be implemented and reactions staged for any security breaches or money laundering attempts. This however is not to be all outsourced for both national and African security reasons. **The Last Digital Frontier** must develop digital warriors especially the youth to be adapt and excellent in cybersecurity so as not to always rely on outsiders for such critical roles whose interests may be contra to the AU or Africapitalism agenda.

The Last Digital Frontier is a leaking ship headed for strong waves surrounded by deep waters and only resolute physical and digital captains who understand what is at stake will assign their warriors to not only find the trojan horses such as the Chinese built African Union headquarters but also annihilate the enemy/intruder while creating the A.I driven threat detection and digital shields fit for the motherland of royalty and her people across the world.

Cointelegraph.com states the most basic definition of blockchain as a shared, digitized ledger that cannot be changed once a transaction has been recorded and verified. According to Wikipedia, Blockchain is a growing list of records, called blocks, which are linked using cryptography; each block containing a cryptographic hash of the previous block,a timestamp, and transaction data and by design a blockchain is resistant to the modification of the data. There are more succinct and complex definitions that I have chosen to ignore for the simpler version here but sites like Blockchain.com, Government Blockchain Association, Akoin.org, BrianAsingia.com among others can provide the necessary details. Blockchain is a critical piece of The Last Digital Frontier e-frastructure (digital infrastructure) as it comes with ideal core African values of trust and transparency (it takes a village). This has strong implications for e-governance (centralized versus decentralized), digital banking across borders, health insurance and service delivery, digital asset ownership and trade from IP to wealth tokenization for land and stocks/shares.

Once The Last Digital Frontier's (IoTs) core digital identity initiative is implemented, ideally on a blockchain backed by A.I for threat detection, logistics both at ports and across borders especially to enforce the AfCFTA is the ideal and starting use case. Longterm, African stock markets and exchange(s) need to be consolidated first through streamlined cross listing and gradually via market or service specialization to increase both the liquidity and volume of transactions. There is ample room for blockchain based exchanges for all kinds of digitized assets across the continent that would deliver not only better transparency and trust but also the necessary transaction volumes and inclusion for both African and foreign investors (household/individual or institutional) to nature a long term investment culture with accessible wealth creation and growth options.

A quick example of successful e-governance innovations is Taiwan's digital minister and his GOV ZERO initiative, Estonia's e-stonia (digital e-citizen) project for business creation by non citizens among other global and African blockchain efforts. Service delivery on a blockchain is for budgeting, mining (resource tracking), taxation (illicit funds flow), health drug trials, cross border trade and logistics as well as policy implementation including census and elections. Land/real estate ownership, communal land for cooperatives, insurance, pensions and savings could all lead to not just financial inclusion through digitization but also increased trust in service delivery across Africa and the world. Trust and culture are the new currency and a blockchain solution backed by A.I is the vault suitable for **The Last Digital Frontier.**

Chapter 16: AOL 2.0 – Africa Online Lives to Become the King of the Digital Economy

A strong African base of security, food, health and education can only be complimented by structurally strong and competitive capital markets (futures, stocks, bonds, ETFs, Funds) as well as exchange(s), pension funds, insurance, legal, IP enforcement and automation of the operations backed by business continuity planning for resilience of service delivery at scale for local effectiveness and global competitiveness.

Foreign businesses with subsidiaries in Africa or main sourcing in Africa are now hot on global exchanges and private equity communities with Jumia, Andela, Flutterwave among others leading the pack. These new pseudo monopolies with global rights and protection unlike local firms enjoy preference like colonial monopolies in energy, mining, telecoms and oil. The future mandates a flip of this equation as China has so that more value addition happens within Africa and capitalization structures favour Africans (51-70% equity with majority ownership at exit) or listing (ideally on a single African exchange) that can be incentivised with deferred taxation policies and complimentary brand exposure as #MadeInAfrica or #DreamAfrica brands, businesses true to Africapitalism.

What Dangote has achieved in food, cement, and now oil with construction heavy jobs in the latter and large operation jobs in the former (ideal) should be replicated across Africa as a direct opposition to EU/US/China policies that seek Africa's continued colonisation through innovation centre construction and operation by westerners as proposed by Germany's Africa Commissioner, Gunter Nooke [BBC] an unsuccessful and un African effort as seen in South Africa with its apartheid based economics having stagnated the countries growth and sidelining the majority of the population in favor of a minority of corporations and old money families.

Beyond education that supports both creative and digital innovations including STEAM programs, financial and legal protection with funding and IP enforcement at local, national, continental and global levels. Digital education backed by commercialization training and programs for school and community innovations is a must. Creativity, ownership and identity can be and must be embedded in innovation.

As articulated by Aliko Dangote in a conversation with Mo Ibrahim on the AfCFTA, Africa has both the youth talent (human capital) and market for its innovations with the global Diaspora and world as secondary markets for the surplus (exports). What is missing from the equation as articulated by 2018 African Union Chair and President of Rwanda, H.E Paul Kagame is more Africans than colonial loyalists i.e political and individual will from leaders at all stages of innovation and governance both public and private to not only sign on, ratify but actually execute and effectively implement the AU reforms and agendas. Those not doing the agreed to reforms are enemies of true and meaningful African progress siding instead with loyalty to colonial statehood only.

Strength in numbers and unity, Umoja as well the Ubuntu philosophy should be embraced across borders and cultures as in the time of our ancestors when Africans of all shapes, cultures and beliefs roomed, moved freely across the motherland to grow, connect and make a better life for themselves and the continent.

To this end, a silo's based innovation culture that extends colonial divide and conquer policies based on fear and hatred needs to be replaced by open, transparent and mostly decentralized and localized innovation and service delivery across borders, languages and cultures except where centralized vs decentralized digital architecture delivers faster, secure and effective service delivery at scale.

The beauty of science and technology is that it allows us to imagine a better world and offer a path forward towards that safer, healthier, wealthier world. This digital world is also borderless as our ancestors lived and to achieve the Africa we want, a new generation of thinking that embraces the African (our ancestors way not the colonial narrative) context is needed.

The Last Digital Frontier State of the Union

*Foreign Influence via Economic, Political, Religious,
Physical and Cyber Military Presence at Scale is a Threat.
(Source: Assenna.com)*

The Eyes in the Sky, Boots on the Ground US Policy Must be Matched and Leveraged or Hedged by the AU (Source: irinews).

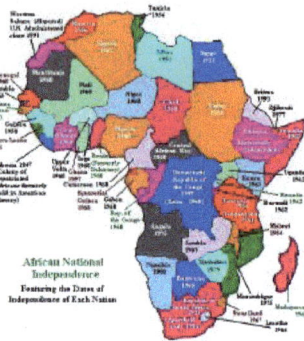

African Independence or the Illusion is a Work in Progress (Source: Wikimedia).

Here and in the rest of the book we delve deeper into the AU Agenda 2063, highlighting its principals, expectations, plans and outcomes as well as the role to be played by Africans within Africa and the Global Diaspora alongside the global community. Afterall, the devil is in the details and as such, verbatim excerpts and AU analysis and reports are shared with complementary analysis for an inside look into the foundation, hopes and dreams of The Last Digital Frontier. Explicit and implicit action plans and their expected results are shared for all of us to find our area of challenge and opportunity so as to forge forward with a single vision.

Agenda 2063: The Africa We Want [au.int overview].

AGENDA 2063 is Africa's blueprint and master plan for transforming Africa into the global powerhouse of the future. It is the continent's strategic framework that aims to deliver on its goal for inclusive and sustainable development and is a concrete manifestation of the pan-African drive for unity, self-determination, freedom, progress and collective prosperity pursued under Pan-Africanism and African Renaissance. The genesis of Agenda 2063 was the realisation by African leaders that there was a need to refocus and prioritise Africa's agenda from the struggle against apartheid and the attainment of political independence for the continent which had been the focus of The Organisation of African Unity (OAU), the precursor of the African Union; and instead to prioritise inclusive social and economic development, continental and regional integration, democratic governance and peace and security amongst other issues aimed at repositioning Africa to becoming a dominant player in the global arena.

As an affirmation of their commitment to support Africa's new path for attaining inclusive and sustainable economic growth and development, African heads of state and government signed the 50th Anniversary Solemn Declaration during the Golden Jubilee celebrations of the formation of the OAU /AU in May 2013. The declaration marked the re-dedication of Africa towards the attainment of the Pan African Vision of "**An integrated, prosperous and peaceful Africa, driven by its own citizens,**

representing a dynamic force in the international arena" and **Agenda 2063 is the concrete manifestation of how the continent intends to achieve this vision within a 50 year period from 2013 to 2063.** The Africa of the future was captured in a letter presented by the former Chairperson of the African Union Commission, Dr. Nkosazana Dlaminin Zuma.

The need to envision a long-term 50 year development trajectory for Africa is important as Africa needs to revise and adapt its development agenda due to ongoing structural transformations; increased peace and reduction in the number of conflicts; renewed economic growth and social progress; the need for people centered development, gender equality and youth empowerment; changing global contexts such as increased globalization and the ICT revolution; the increased unity of Africa which makes it a global power to be reckoned with and capable of rallying support around its own common agenda; and emerging development and investment opportunities in areas such as agri-business, infrastructure development, health and education as well as the value addition in African commodities

Agenda 2063 encapsulates not only Africa's Aspirations for the Future but also identifies key Flagship Programmes which can boost Africa's economic growth and development and lead to the rapid transformation of the continent.

Agenda 2063 also identifies key activities to be undertaken in its 10 year Implementation Plans which will ensure that Agenda 2063 delivers both quantitative and qualitative Transformational Outcomes for Africa's people. [au.int]

The African Union, Digitized for You [au.int]

The AU Agenda 2063 is ambitious but needs a detailed analysis of the status, challenges and opportunities with an urgent call to action to act now not later. The First Ten Year Implementation Plan (FTYIP) of Agenda 2063 (2013 – 2023) is the first in a series of five ten year plans over the fifty year horizon of Agenda

2063's 50 time frame.

The purpose for developing the ten year plans are to [au.int ftyip]:
Identify priority areas, set specific targets, define strategies and policy measures required to implement the FTYIP of Agenda 2063.
Bring to fruition the Fast Track programmes and initiatives outlined in the Malabo Decisions of the African Union (AU) to provide the big push and breakthroughs for Africa's economic and social transformation.
Provide information to all key stakeholders at the national, regional and continental levels on the expected results / outcomes for the first ten years of the plan and assign responsibilities to all stakeholders in its implementation, monitoring and evaluation
Outline the strategies required to ensure availability of resources and capacities together with citizen's engagement in the implementation of the First Ten Year Plan.
To ensure that Agenda 2063 is not only implemented but that it has measurable results, the FTYIP enumerates 20 Agenda 2063 Goals linked to the 7 Aspiration and each of these goals identifies the priority areas to be implemented at a national level to ensure that collectively Africa will attain its developmental objectives. The goals and priority areas of the FTYIP were influenced by 4 key factors:

The Flagship Projects /Programmes of
Agenda 2063
Near Term National and Regional
Economic Communities (RECs)
Development Priorities
Continental Frameworks:
Agenda 2063 Results Framework

Member State Profiles
(*) Represents Member States under political
sanction

On May 25 1963 in Addis Ababa, Ethiopia, the
32 African states that had achieved independence
at that time agreed to establish the Organization
of African Unity (OAU). A further 21 members
joined gradually, reaching a total of 53 by the
time of the AU's creation in 2002. There are 55
Member States. The following list shows all
members, in alphabetical order, and their date of
joining the AU or its predecessor the OAU
[au.int].

Format: **Name Capital   Calling Code
Currency   Independence Day   Head of
Government Head of State**
People's Democratic Republic of Algeria
People's Democratic Republic of Algeria
Algiers+213   Algerian Dinar (DZD)July 05,
1962   Prime Minister Ahmed Ouyahia   H.E.
M. Abdelkader Bensalah

Republic of Angola   Republic of Angola
Luanda+244   Kwanza (AOA)   November
11, 1975   Vice President Bornito de Sousa
Baltazar Diogo   President Joao Lourenzo
Republic of Benin   Republic of Benin
Porto-Novo   +229   CFA franc(XOF)
August 01, 1960   President Mr
Patrice Talon
Republic of Botswana Republic of Botswana
Gaborone   +267   Pula (BWP)   September
30, 1966   President Mokgweetsi
Masisi
Burkina Faso   Burkina Faso   Ouagadougou
+226   West African CFA franc (XOF)
August 05, 1960   Prime Minister Paul Kaba
Thieba President Roch Marc Kabore
Republic of Burundi   Republic of Burundi
Bujumbura   +257   Burundi franc (FBu)(BIF)
        July 01, 1962   President Pierre
Nkurunziza
Republic of Cameroon   Republic of
Cameroon   Yaounde   +237   CFA franc
(XAF) January 01, 1960   Prime Minister
Philémon Yang   President Paul Biya
Republic of Cabo Verde   Republic of Cabo
Verde   Praia   +238   Cape verdean escudo
(CVE) July 05, 1975   Prime Minister Ulisses
Correia e SilvaPresident Jorge Carlos Fonseca
* Central African Republic   * Central African
Republic   Bangui +236   Central african
CFA franc (XAF)   August 13, 1960

Prime Minister Simplice Sarandji   President
Faustin A. Touadera
The Republic of Chad,   The Republic of
Chad   N'Djamena   +235   CFA franc (XAF)
        August 11, 1960   Prime Minister
Albert Pahimi Padacké   President Idriss
Déby
Union of the ComorosUnion of the Comoros
Moroni   +269   Comorian franc (KMF)
        July 06, 1975   President Azali
Assoumane
Republic of the Congo   Republic of the
Congo Brazzaville   +242   Central African
CFA franc   August 15, 1960   Prime
Clement Mouamba   President Denis
Sassou-Nguesso
Republic of Cote d'Ivoire   Republic of Cote
d'Ivoire   Yamoussoukro   +225
CFA franc (XOF)   August 07, 1960
Prime Minister Amadou Gon Coulibaly
President Alassane Dramane Ouattara
Democratic Republic of the Congo   Democratic
Republic of the Congo   Kinshasa
+243   Congolese franc (CDF)   June 30,
1960   Prime Minister Bruno Tshibala
President Joseph Kabila
Republic of Djibouti   Republic of Djibouti
Djibouti   +253   Franc (DJF)   June 27,
1977   Prime Minister Abdoukader Kamil
Mohamed   President Ismail Omar Guelleh
Arab Republic of Egypt   Arab Republic of

Egypt   Cairo   +20   Egyptian pound (EGP)
February 28, 1922   Prime Minister
Sherif Ismail   President Abdel Fatah el-Sisi
Republic of Equatorial Guinea   Republic of
Equatorial Guinea   Malabo   +240
CFA franc   October 12, 1968   Prime
Minister Francisco Pascual Obama Asue
President Obiang Nguema Mbasogo
State of Eritrea   State of Eritrea
Asmara   +291   Nakfa (ERN)   May 24,
1993   President Isaias Afewerki
Federal Democratic Republic of Ethiopia
Federal Democratic Republic of Ethiopia
Addis Ababa   +251   Birr   Prime
Minister Abiy Ahmed Ali   President Mulatu
Teshome
Gabonese Republic   Gabonese Republic
Libreville   +241   CFA franc   August 17,
1960   Prime Minister Emmanuel Issozé
Ngondet   President Ali Ben Bongo
Republic of the Gambia   Republic of the
Gambia   Banjul +220   Dalasi (GMD)
February 18, 1965   President Adama
Barrow
Republic of Ghana   Republic of Ghana
Accra +233   Ghanaian cedi(GHC) March 06,
1957   President Nana Akufo-Addo
Republic of Guinea   Republic of Guinea
Conakry   +224   Guinean franc (GNF)
October 02, 1958   Prime Minister Mohamed
Said Fofana   President Alpha Condé

Republic of Guinea-Bissau   Republic of
Guinea-Bissau Bissau +245   CFA franc (XOF)
        September 24, 1973   Prime Minister
H.E. Mr Umaro El Mokhtar Sissoco Embalo
President Jose Mario Vaz
Republic of Kenya   Republic of Kenya
Nairobi   +254   Kenyan shilling (KES)
        December 12, 1963   Deputy President
William Ruto President Uhuru Muigai Kenyatta
Kingdom of Lesotho   Kingdom of Lesotho
Maseru+266   Loti (LSL)   October 04, 1966
        Prime Minister Thomas Thabane
King Letsie III
Republic of Liberia   Republic of Liberia
Monrovia   +231   Liberian Dollar(LRD) July
26, 1847   President Ellen
Johnson-Sirleaf
Libya   Libya   Tripoli +218   Lybian
Dinar(LYD)   December 24, 1951   Prime
Minister Fayez el-Sarraj   President
Mohammed El-Megaref
Republic of Madagascar   Republic of
Madagascar   Antananarivo +261   Malagasy
ariay(MGA)   June 26, 1960 Prime Minister
Olivier Mahafaly Solonandrasana   H. E. Mr
Hery Martial Rakotoarimanana
Rajaonarimampianina
Republic of Malawi   Republic of Malawi
Lilongwe   +265   Kwacha(D)(MWK)   July
06, 1964   Vice President Saulos Chilima
        President Peter Muharika

Republic of Mali   Republic of Mali
Bamako   +223   CFA franc (XOF)
September 22, 1960   Prime Minister Modibo
Keita   President Ibrahim Boubakar Keita
Republic of Mauritania   Republic of
Mauritania   Nouakchott   +222   Mauritanian
Ouguiya (MRO)   November 28, 1960
Prime Minister Yahya Ould Hademine
President Mohamed Ould Abdel Aziz
Republic of Mauritius Republic of Mauritius Port
Louis +230   Mauritian rupee (MUR)
March 12, 1968   Prime Minister Mr.
Pravind Kumar Jugnauth   President Ameenah
Gurib-Fakim
Kingdom of Morocco Rabat +212   Moroccan
Dirham   April 07, 1956 Prime Minister
Saad-Eddine El Othmani   King Mohammed
VI
Republic of Mozambique   Republic of
Mozambique   Maputo   +258
Mozambican metical (Mtn) (MZN)   June 25,
1975   Prime Minister Carlos Agostinho. do
Rosario   President Filipe Nyusi
Republic of Namibia   Republic of Namibia
Windhoek   +264   Namibian dollar(NAD)
        March 21, 1990   Prime Minister
Saara Kungongelwa A.   President Hage
Geingob
Republic of Niger   Republic of Niger
Niamey   +227   CFA franc (XOF)
August 03, 1960   Prime Minister Brigi

Rafini President Mohamadou Issoufou
Federal Republic of Nigeria   Federal Republic
of Nigeria   Abuja +234   Nigerian naira and
Kobo(NGN)   October 01, 1960
President Muhammadu Buhari
Republic of Rwanda   Republic of Rwanda
Kigali +250   Rwandan franc(RWF)July 01,
1962   Prime Minister H.E. Mr Edouard
Ngirente   President Paul Kagame
Republic Arab Saharawi Democratic Saharawi
Arab Democratic Republic   Aauin
saharawi pesetas   February 27, 1976
          President Brahim Ghali
Democratic Republic of sao Tome and Principe
          Democratic Republic of sao Tome and
Principe   Sao Tome   +239
Dobra(STD)   July 12, 1975 Prime Minister
Patrice Emery Trovoada   President Manuel
Pinto Da Costa
Republic of Senegal   Republic of Senegal
Dakar +221   CFA franc(XOF)   June 20,
1960   Prime Minister Mohamed Ben Adallah
DionnePresident Macky Sall
Republic of Seychelles   Republic of
Seychelles   Victoria   +248   Seychellois
rupee(SCR)   June 29, 1976   President
Danny Faure
Republic of Sierra Leone   Republic of Sierra
Leone Freetown   +232   Leone (SLL)
April 27, 1961 H.E Mohammed Juldeh Jallow
          H.E. Julius Maada Bio

Somali Republic   Somali Republic
Mogadishu   +252   Somali shilling (SOS) July
01, 1960   Prime Minister H.E. Mr Hassan
Ali Kheyre   President H.E. Mr Mohamed
Abdullahi Farmajo
Republic of South Africa   Republic of South
Africa Pretoria (Executive), Bloemfontein
(Judical), CapeTown (Legislative)   +27
South African rand (ZAR)   April 27, 1994
        President Jacob Zuma
Republic of South Sudan   Republic of South
Sudan Juba   +211   South Sudanese Pound
        July 09, 2011   President Salva Kir
Republic of The Sudan   Republic of The
Sudan Khartoum   +249   Sudanese pound
(SDG,SDD)   January 01, 1956
President Omar al-Bashir
Kingdom of Swaziland   Kingdom of
Swaziland   Lobamba(royal and legislative)
Mbabane (Administrative)   +268
Lilangeni(SZL)   September 06, 1968
Prime Minister Barnabas Sibusiso Dlamini
King Mswati III
United Republic of Tanzania United Republic of
Tanzania   Dar es Salaam(traditional capital)
Dodoma (Location of legislature)   +255
Tanzanian shilling (TZS)   December 09, 1961
        Prime Minister Kassim Majaliwa
President John Magufuli
Togolese Republic   Togolese Republic
Lome` +228   CFA franc (XOF)   April 27,

1960   Prime Minister Selom Komi Klassou
President Faure Gnassingbé
Tunisian Republic   Tunisian Republic
Tunis +216   Tunisian dinar(TND) March 20,
1956   Prime Minister Youssef Chahed
President Beji Caid Essebsi
Republic of Uganda   Republic of Uganda
Kampala   +256   Ugandan shilling (UGX)
          October 09, 1962   Prime Minister
Ruhakana Rugunba   President Yoweri
Museveni
Republic of Zambia   Republic of Zambia
Lusaka+260   Zambian Kwacha(ZMK)
October 24, 1964   Vice President Inongue
Winta President Edgar Lungu
Republic of Zimbabwe   Republic of
Zimbabwe   Harare +263   Zimbabwe
Dollars(ZW$) April 18, 1980   President
Emmerson Dambudzo Mnangagwa

Also important is how the AU is funded.
Financing of the Union is a historic decision
adopted by Heads of State and Government
(HOSG) in a "Retreat on Financing of the
Union" during the 27th African Union Summit
held in Kigali, Rwanda in July 2016. The
Decision directs all African Union Member
States to implement a 0.2% levy on eligible
imports for to finance the African Union. The
Retreat was attended by Heads of State and
Government, Ministers of Foreign

Affairs, Ministers of Finance and other representatives of Member States. The High Representative on the Peace Fund Dr. Donald Kaberuka presented comprehensive proposals on financing the Union including the Peace Fund [au.int au financing].

On the Financing of the Union:
i) To institute and implement a 0.2 percent Levy on all eligible imported
goods into the Continent to finance the African Union Operational ,
Program and Peace Support Operations Budgets starting from the
year 2017;
ii) That the amounts collected from the Levy shall be automatically paid
by the national administration, into an account opened for the African
Union with the Central Banks of each Member State for transmission
to the African Union in accordance with each Member State's
assessed contribution;
iii) That the Commission shall put in place strong oversight and
accountability mechanisms for ensuring the effective and prudent use
of the resources;
iv) That the Commission should complete the on-going institutional

reform of the African Union to ensure a more effective attainment of
the objective of the Union and prudent use of all resources;
v) To establish a Committee of Ministers of Finance comprising [ten]
Member States, representing the five (5) regions [two per region] to
participate in the preparation of the annual budget.

The following list covers external partnerships where there are formal agreements between the AU and a partner organisation, region or country [au.int partnerships].

Africa–Arab Partnership Formal relations between Africa and the Arab World were launched at a summit in Cairo, Egypt, in 1977 and revitalised at a summit in Sirte, Libya, in 2010. The Libya Summit adopted the Africa–Arab Partnership Strategy and the Joint Africa–Arab Action Plan 2011–16 as well as issuing a declaration summarising common positions on major regional and international issues. The Partnership's focal areas are: trade; mining and industry; agriculture; energy and water resources; transport and communication; financial cooperation; and educational, scientific and technical cooperation. The Partnership's core structures as set out in the Strategy are a standing commission, working groups and specialised panels, coordinating committee, ad hoc court and Commission of Conciliation and Arbitration. The Joint Africa–Arab Heads of State and Government Summit is held every three years with ministerial-level meetings every 18 months. As of September 2014, three Africa–Arab joint summits have been held, most recently on 19 and 20 November 2013 in Kuwait.

Africa–European Union (EU) Partnership Internet: www.africa-eu-partnership.org The Africa–EU Partnership began with the first Africa–EU Summit, which was held in 2000 in Cairo, Egypt. As of September 2014, four summits have been held, most recently on 2 and 3 April 2014 in Brussels, Belgium. The Partnership's stated vision is to: reinforce political relations; strengthen and promote issues of common concern; promote effective multilateralism; and promote people-centred partnerships. Activities are based on the Joint Africa–Europe Strategy, which was adopted by Heads of State and Government at the 2007 Summit, and the Joint Road Map 2014–17, which was adopted at the April 2014 Summit. Partnership mechanisms operate at a range of levels from Heads of State summits to civil society networks.

Africa–South America (ASA) Summit

The first ASA Summit was held in November 2006 in Abuja, Nigeria. As of September 2014, three summits have been held, most recently in February 2013 in Malabo, Equatorial Guinea. The Summit's mandate is to facilitate the development of trade and industry for both regions, including through sharing best practices in priority thematic areas. The Summit is also a forum for dialogue on peace and security, democracy, governance and social justice. The ASA Summit's core structures under development include a strategic presidential committee, permanent secretariat and executive secretary. A financing mechanism for partnership programmes is also under development.

Africa–India The Africa–India Cooperation Agreement was launched by a leaders' summit in April 2008 in New Delhi, India. The Summit adopted two documents: the Delhi Declaration and an Africa– India Framework for Cooperation. A second summit was held on 25 May 2011 in Addis Ababa, Ethiopia, and a third was scheduled to be held in December 2014. The first four-year Africa– India Plan of Action (2010–13) was launched in New Delhi in March 2010 and a second was adopted in Addis Ababa in September 2013 for 2014–18. The Plan includes cooperation in the economic, political, science and technology, social development and capacity building, tourism, energy, infrastructure and media fields.

Africa–Turkey The Africa–Turkey Partnership was formalised in April 2008 at the Istanbul Summit. The 2008 Summit adopted two outcome documents, the Istanbul Declaration and the Framework for Cooperation, which set out the areas of cooperation between the two parties. The Framework's focal areas are: inter-governmental cooperation; trade and investment; agriculture, agribusiness, rural development, water resources management and small- and medium-scale enterprises; health; peace and security; infrastructure, energy and transport; culture, tourism and education; media, information and communication technology; and environment. An implementation plan for 2010–14 was adopted in 2010. The second Africa– Turkey Summit was scheduled to take place in November 2014.

China–Africa Cooperation Forum (FOCAC) The China–Africa Cooperation Forum is a ministerial-level platform for consultation and dialogue between China and African states. It was inaugurated in October 2000 in Beijing, China. In addition to the Member States, the AU Commission is a full member. The Forum is mandated to strengthen consultation, expand cooperation and promote political dialogue and economic cooperation between China and

African states. FOCAC conferences are held every three years, alternating between China and an African country. FOCAC has held five sessions since the inaugural meeting in Beijing, most recently on 19 and 20 July 2012 in Beijing. The next FOCAC meeting is scheduled for 2015.

Africa–United States The African Union and United States of America (USA) signed an assistance agreement in August 2010. The Agreement formalised cooperation on issues including peace and security, democracy and governance, agriculture, health, trade and general capacity building. The USA and AU held an inaugural high-level meeting in 2010 as a platform to bring together cabinet- level officials. An Africa–USA Summit was held in August 2014 in Washington, DC, under the theme "Invest in the future".

Tokyo International Conference on African Development (TICAD) Africa–Japan cooperation was formalised in 1993 by the Tokyo International Conference on African Development (TICAD), which established a consultative forum for development assistance to Africa. TICAD meets at Heads of State and Government level every five years, most recently in June 2013 in Yokohama, Japan. The most recent ministerial meeting took place in May 2014, in Yaoundé, Cameroon. The AU

Commission became a full partner of the TICAD process at the TICAD IV forum in 2008 and a forum co-organiser from 2012. TICAD is overseen by a follow-up mechanism, which comprises a three-tier structure of secretariat, joint monitoring committee and follow-up meeting. Each TICAD meeting approves an action plan with specific actions to be undertaken within a five-year period.

Africa–Korea The Korea–Africa Forum was established at the first ministerial-level Korea–Africa Forum, which was held in November 2006 in Seoul, Republic of Korea. Since then, the Forum has been held every three years, most recently in October 2012 in Seoul. The Ministerial Forum meets to discuss major economic development issues. Meetings include academics and the business sector from both sides of the partnership. A consultative group manages the partnership. It is composed of African Development Bank executive directors, senior African and Republic of Korea Government officials and the Export-Import Bank of Korea. A secretariat is drawn from the same bodies.

Africa–Australia The Africa–Australia partnership was formalised by a memorandum of understanding (MoU) in September 2010. The MoU establishes a framework for cooperation between Australia and the AU Commission. It prioritises cooperation in relation to: trade and investment; peace and security; achievement of the Millennium Development Goals; agriculture and food security; democracy, governance and human rights; and climate change.

The individual AU frameworks below are where the pilot projects are launched in coordination with global and regional strategic partners:

- Comprehensive African Agricultural Development Programme (CAADP)
- The Programme for Infrastructural Development in Africa (PIDA)
- The African Mining Vision (AMV)
- Science Technology Innovation Strategy for Africa (STISA)
- Boosting Intra African Trade (BIAT)
- Accelerated Industrial Development for Africa (AIDA)

The Individual in The Last Digital Frontier

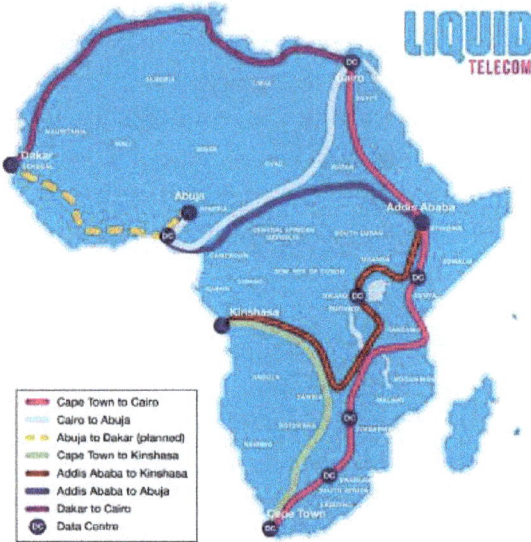

Liquid Telecom, an Econet Wireless Subsidiary is Leading African Owned Digital Transformation (Source: LiquidNet).

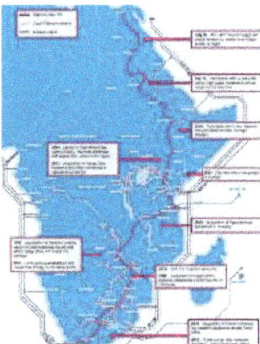

Econet is a Nigerian Company founded by Zimbean and London based Strive Masiyiwa after his own government was threatened by his passion for connecting and digitizing Africa to the point that he self exiled himself due to the threats from contesting government monopoly on communications while under serving the public with a few landlines.

Identity and in particular digital identities are the key to foundational peace and security in Africa as well as the innovation and wealth ownership that results. According to CNN, Microsoft is also confident the use of their blockchain for digital identity could lead to "tens of thousands" of operations per second, an improvement to the Bitcoin and Blockchain frameworks. In a blog post, the tech giant explained:

> "We believe every person needs a decentralized, digital identity they own and control, backed by self-owned identifiers that enable secure, privacy-preserving interactions. This self-owned identity must seamlessly integrate into their lives and put them at the center of everything they do in the digital world."

> A blockchain identity would allow people to log into online accounts without having to reaffirm themselves each time. As it stands, multiple online accounts mean multiple logins. A blockchain-based digital identity would allow users to simply log in once and then use that ID to access their online data, reducing "pain points," as Microsoft calls them.

For Microsoft, the move likely means two things, the first being that they are looking to accomplish what several other companies either haven't or couldn't in the past. The second thing is that Microsoft clearly views blockchain as a technology that's not part of the future but rather already here. [CNN, Microsoft Blockchain]

Agenda 2063 seeks to deliver on a set of Seven Aspirations each with its own set of goals which if achieved will move Africa closer to achieving its vision for the year 2063. These 7 Aspirations reflect our desire for shared prosperity and well-being, for unity and integration, for a continent of free citizens and expanded horizons, where the full potential of women and youth are realised, and with freedom from fear, disease and want [Au.int].

Aspiration 1: A prosperous Africa based on inclusive growth and sustainable development.

We are determined to eradicate poverty in one generation and build shared prosperity through social and economic transformation of the continent.

Goals:
A high standard of living, quality of life and well-being for all through ending poverty, inequalities of income and opportunity; job creation, especially addressing youth unemployment; facing up to the challenges of rapid population growth and urbanization, improvement of habitats and access to basic necessities of life – water, sanitation, electricity; providing social security and protection;

Well educated citizens and skills revolutions underpinned by science, technology and innovation and developing Africa's human and social capital (through an education and skills revolution emphasizing science and technology);

Healthy and well-nourished citizens by expanding access to quality health care services, particularly for women and girls;

Transformed economies and jobs by transforming Africa's economies through beneficiation from Africa's natural resources, manufacturing, industrialization and value addition, as well as raising productivity and competitiveness;

Modern agriculture for increased proactivity and production by radically transforming African agriculture to enable the continent to feed itself and be a major player as a net food exporter;

Blue/Ocean Economy for accelerated economic growth by exploiting the vast potential of Africa's blue/ocean economy;

Environmentally sustainable climate and resilient economies and communities by putting in place measures to sustainably manage the continent's rich biodiversity, forests, land and waters and using mainly adaptive measures to address climate change risks.

Aspiration 2: An integrated continent, politically united and based on the ideals of Pan-Africanism and the vision of Africa's Renaissance.

Since 1963, the quest for African Unity has been inspired by the spirit of Pan Africanism, focusing on liberation, and political and economic independence. It is motivated by development based on self-reliance and self-determination of African people, with democratic and people-centred governance.

Goals:

United Africa (Federal/Confederate) by accelerating progress towards continental unity and integration for sustained growth, trade, exchanges of goods, services, free movement of people and capital through establishing a United Africa and fast tracking economic integration through the establishment of the AfCFTA;

World class infrastructure criss-crosses Africa by improving connectivity through newer and bolder initiatives to link the continent by rail, road, sea and air; and developing regional and continental power pools, as well as ICT;

Decolonisation where all remnants of colonialism will have ended and all African territories under occupation fully liberated. We shall take measures to expeditiously end the unlawful occupation of the Chagos Archipelago, the Comorian Island of Mayotte and affirming the right to self-determination of the people of Western Sahara.

Aspiration 3: An Africa of good governance, democracy, respect for human rights, justice and the rule of law.

An Africa of good governance, democracy, respect for human rights, justice and the rule of law. Africa shall have a universal culture of good governance, democratic values, gender equality, and respect for human rights, justice and the rule of law.

> Goals:
> Democratic values, practices, universal principles for human rights, justice and the rule of law entrenched by consolidating democratic gains and improving the quality of governance, respect for human rights and the rule of law;
> Capable institutions and transformed leadership in place at all levels by building strong institutions for a development state; and facilitating the emergence of development-oriented and visionary leadership in all spheres and at all levels.

Aspiration 4: A peaceful and secure Africa

Mechanisms for peaceful prevention and resolution of conflicts will be functional at all levels. As a first step, dialogue-centred conflict prevention and resolution will be actively promoted in such a way that by 2020 all guns will be silent. A culture of peace and tolerance shall be nurtured in Africa's children and youth through peace education.

> Goals:
> Peace security and stability is preserved by strengthening governance, accountability and transparency as a foundation for a peaceful Africa;
> A stable and peaceful Africa by strengthening mechanisms for securing peace and reconciliation at

all levels, as well as addressing emerging threats to
Africa's peace and security;
A fully functional and operational APSA by putting
in place strategies for the continent to finance her
security needs.

Aspiration 5: An Africa with a strong cultural identity,
common heritage, shared values and ethics

Pan-Africanism and the common history, destiny,
identity, heritage, respect for religious diversity and
consciousness of African people's and her diaspora's will be
entrenched.

Goal:
Africa cultural renaissance is pre-eminent by
inculcating the spirit of Pan Africanism; tapping
Africa's rich heritage and culture to ensure that the
creative arts are major contributors to Africa's growth
and transformation; and restoring and preserving
Africa's cultural heritage, including its languages.

Aspiration 6: An Africa, whose development is people-driven,
relying on the potential of African people, especially its
women and youth, and caring for children.

All the citizens of Africa will be actively involved in
decision making in all aspects. Africa shall be an inclusive
continent where no child, woman or man will be left behind
or excluded, on the basis of gender, political affiliation,
religion, ethnic affiliation, locality, age or other factors.

Goals:
Full gender equality in all spheres of life by

strengthening the role of Africa's women through ensuring gender equality and parity in all spheres of life (political, economic and social); eliminating all forms of discrimination and violence against women and girls;

Engaged and empowered youth and children by creating opportunities for Africa's youth for self-realisation, access to health, education and jobs; ensuring safety and security for Africa's children, and providing for early childhood development.

Aspiration 7: Africa as a strong, united, resilient and influential global player and partner.

Africa shall be a strong, united, resilient, peaceful and influential global player and partner with a significant role in world affairs. We affirm the importance of African unity and solidarity in the face of continued external interference including, attempts to divide the continent and undue pressures and sanctions on some countries.

Goals:

Africa as a major partner in global affairs and peaceful co-existence by improving Africa's place in the global governance system (UN Security Council, financial institutions, global commons such as outer space);

Africa takes full responsibility for financing her development by improving Africa's partnerships and refocusing them more strategically to respond to African priorities for growth and transformation; and ensuring that the continent has the right strategies to finance its own development and reducing aid dependency.

Individual aspirations, responsibility and accountability are the missing link in Agenda 2063's success. The AU commission is trying and making good progress but individuals must step up and not only learn, participate but also lead the AU efforts. With great power comes great responsibility and as such, every African must be ready to take responsibility for their aspirations, priorities, votes, and leadership decisions. This can then translate to actual prosecution of corrupt individuals and removal of power of corrupt leaders rather than hiding behind institutions, political parties and religion. Individuals not systems or vacuums make decisions and choices that have short term and long term impacts. Our choice to embrace and support Agenda 2063 will determine the Africa we get. Will it be the Africa you want, the Africa we want or the Africa they want? What if some individual values aligned with others and together we realized #theAfricaWeWant? The answer you and I seek starts with each of us, owning our dreams and actions/choices starting today because every dream, choice and story matters. What is your dream/story?

The Family in The Last Digital Frontier

Automation and Robotics bring creative destruction. African families must embrace the future and create it by preparing today. Not everyone needs to be a doctor or lawyer, but should nature creative design and culture (Source: Visual Capitalist)

Financial Literacy and Inclusion a Day One Priority

The Family becomes the success cornerstone of Agenda 2063. If the individual through belief, training, execution and trade realises agenda 2063, it is the family that sustains it across generations. From early childhood education to food security, job creation and actualization, savings, investments and civic engagement, the family is the ultimate beneficiary of a successful social economic campaign. As in many cultures and religions and indeed the modern state, the family should receive the protection, benefits and opportunities it needs to thrive. The family and its role extends beyond lifestyle choices and should extend to the health, education, work, savings and investments roles in addition to political or civic engagement.

Financial decisions around home ownership, land ownership and the necessary savings from jobs as well as investment planning can be digitized both for planning and realization purposes. Such decision making happens before children become part of the picture but even when children are already, digital identity tools in line with Agenda 2063 would allow for transparent budgeting, goal setting and planning on a family level to compliment the individual goals. Here, wealth transfer, inheritance and other trust based activities can and should be resolved, tracked, valued and settled seamlessly leveraging digital tools in sync with global financial markets.

Family health can and should be a rallying cornerstone to embed agenda 2063 values and aspirations across borders. The right to a healthy environment and lifestyle should be pushed at home, at school and in communities from parents who can be both role models at home but also at work as they influence their networks. Charity begins at home and as such local healthy food options should be supported over unhealthy, processed junk which also has a complimentary benefit of supporting intra Africa Agriculture. Moreover, with children growing up in families with healthy lifestyles, and an awareness of the need for more preventive measures against diseases instead of last minute crisis aversion or management, the children are likely to grow up to use, support and sign effective public health policies, solutions and plans including accessible insurance packages and treatments.

Family education from family values to culture and "religion" can be a strong foundation for raising an ethically responsible future generation both at home and at school. The role of family in African history must take centre stage again to unite and mobilize Africa's human capital towards lifelong learning, resource owning, research and value added production. From local job creation to community input in investment and development projects within their communities, educated families on long term risks and opportunities of projects are more likely to contribute to and sustain projects. Education here does not mean "colonial education" but rather an authentic awareness of Africans of their history, their natural and mineral wealth, their opportunities and leverage against foreign influence as well as the critical challenges of their generation. A culture of celebrating our ancestors accomplishments while embracing our own challenges of our time must be cultivated and natured as opposed to accepting the old guard lifetime leaders as the new normal.

Family civic engagement must be one of hope, preparation and cooperation with an emphasis on security (physical, economic and social) as the foundation for policy. By embracing Agenda 2063 aspirations and adapting them to be family values, families can grow to appreciate their history, culture, challenges and opportunities instead of losing out to sharks and hawkers ready to grab wealth at all costs. From local elections to national campaigns and leadership participation, families should cultivate an openness to civic engagement, support for people first policies and leaders as well as having the will to step in themselves and run for office if they believe and know that they can do a better job. Children must grow up knowing that they can be better leaders than those in power so that succession and Agenda 2063 aspirations become intertwined and not opposites.

Family travel can and should be supported for cultural, educational, economic and civic engagement and knowledge sharing across borders and cultures. Agenda 2063 will only succeed if individuals and families are educated, supported and given opportunities to learn, vote and even run for office and travel can help highlight the similarities and differences in service delivery in other neighbouring states leading to both collaboration and pressure on local leaders to deliver more effectively like their neighbors. As the African saying goes, one who does not travel thinks their mother is the best cook. Families can begin to see through the lies of local politicians and demand more as well as do more for themselves if they realise that this is possible through communities they interact with.

Family taxation and incentives should be modified to incentivise a savings and investment culture as well as local business funding and ownership. The savings and investments provide capital needed for African ventures and projects but investments also provide inclusive access to intra Africa businesses and assets should a pan Africa stock exchange be realized. By complementing such incentives with financial literacy efforts from schools, banks and religious centres, cities and employers will create a more knowledgeable society that makes better socio-economic decisions.

Family businesses for scale is my personal mantra for success in Africa. As business environments are often unfriendly and favor large multinationals over SME's, African family owned businesses have a role to play in Africa's economic development. Beyond understanding local markets better, having a family brand identity as well as deep community relationships, families if managed correctly have a long term intergenerational mandate to prepare for the next generation. Thus savings, investments and growth are ideally long term and leave community interests at heart. There is room to find private equity models that compliment family businesses from family office funds to mergers and acquisitions as well as franchises. Family ownership and wealth creation has to be supported on all fronts so that a network effect and redistribution of wealth is possible at scale beyond corporate tied assets and values. Franchises are one way for intra Africa scale beyond mergers and launches for family owned businesses.

The family as a unit becomes the most logical unit from which to measure Agenda 2063 realizations. Are African families safer, economically included, owning more of their nations wealth, healthier, earning more, saving more, learning better and investing back into their communities? Asking this among other questions can easily drive evaluation processes around policies, projects and political tenures or terms. Indeed individual participation in realizing agenda 2063 through family preparation and support is a stronger bet that throwing all our eggs on some African leaders who are still trapped in the 20th century, unaware of the pressing challenges of our generation as well as the changing global balance of powers. The African family is both local and global and diaspora links should be strengthened through travel, investments and civic engagement.

The Community in The Last Digital Frontier

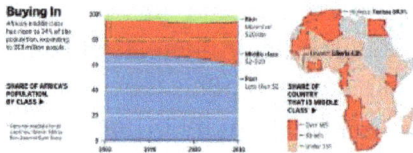

Job creation and retention a major KPI (Source: AfDB).

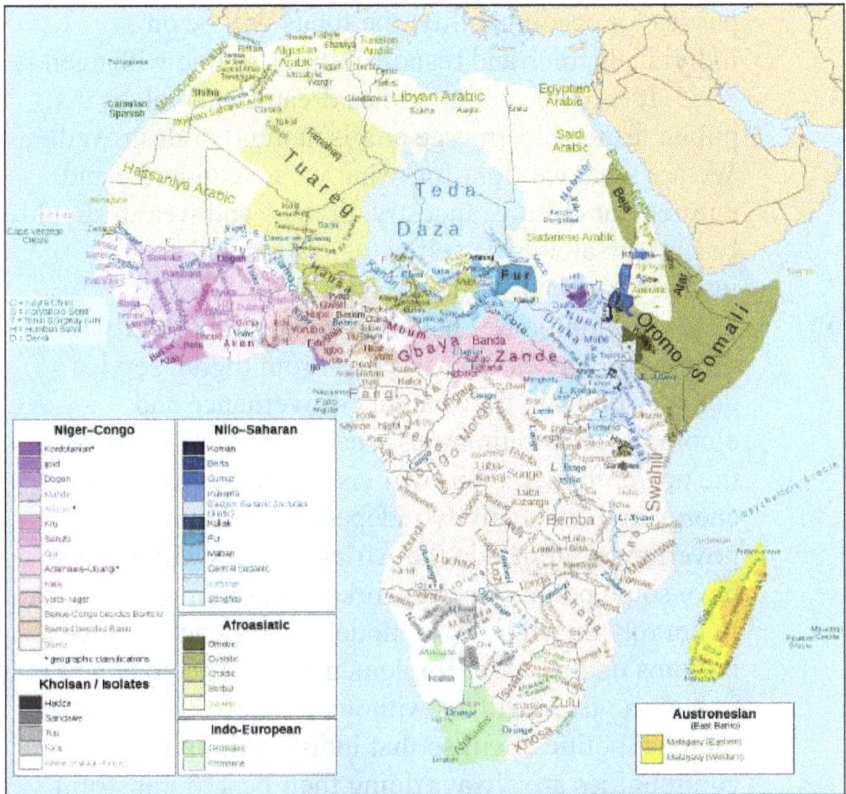

Automated Localization at Scale Critical to Effective Service Delivery and Community Ownership (Source: Wikimedia)

The community shall refer to both the people within spaces (individuals and families as well as visitors) and the physical space they occupy such as villages and town centers or cities (though a special point is made on city and municipal leadership). Because it is ultimately people and in particular individuals that make policies or decisions and are thus the responsible parties for accountability, the focus will be on individuals roles and responsibilities in line with agenda 2063. It is on the communities dreams and values that public leadership emerge and is natured or destroyed. We are what we fight for, what we love, tolerate and nature. Our culture, ancestry, dreams and wealth should be high up alongside self actualisation and intergenerational wealth transfer.

Communities have the unique opportunity to offer new courses for Africans. From digital service delivery pilots to transparent e-governance and e-commerce, communities whether rural or urban have the power to map their own vision including that for energy and connectivity independence. While government alongside the African Union will always have some policies in the works, communities must learn to not rely on a top down model but instead embrace a bottoms up model for implementation. The goal here is to have a vision with or without the lack of national or regional political will so that individuals and communities are always doing their best to transform their social and economic well being. For example, failed schools, power and connectivity initiatives are rampant across Africa and communities must resort to responding to their own community needs with or without the government. Power, connectivity, preventive health and education can be "village projects" that crowd source knowledge, talent and resources to compliment as well as out compete government initiatives.

Local governments should strive for effective service delivery as they are closest to their community members. Members as well should use this proximity to live responsible civic participation such as voting, running for office and enforcing the law including removal of corrupt officials. While corrupt government officials may often bribe, intimidate and pressure local governments to follow the dark path of ineffective service delivery, resistance must be strategic and absolute at all levels from individuals to families and ultimately communities. As seen in Sudan and across many African states both through local or provincial elections as in South Africa or civic engagement as in Rwanda, communities can form positive contributions that compliment and or also exceed national visions.

Communities must fight for environmental and economic inclusivity alongside socio-economic sustainability in all community projects and initiatives. After all, second to human capital, Africa's wealth is in its culture, environment and land including natural resources. These must be guarded for the wealth banks and vaults they are against short term thinking policy makers and politicians who only live to serve economic and political treason. A co-opetion among communities tracked digitally can encourage both friendly collaboration and knowledge/talent exchange while competing for effective service delivery with communities learning from and alongside each other towards effective service delivery.

Intra Africa goals and national agendas must be translated to community needs and values or even better adapted to incorporate community aspirations so that execution ownership and long term wealth and value creation becomes the new norm. This can not and will not happen if government, institutional and policy drafts are contra to urgent people needs and dreams such as the need for reliable power, connectivity and economic inclusion in Nigeria failed by strong reliance on inefficient banking systems stuck in the 20th century with minimal inclusive innovations for all Nigerians.

Berber/Amazigh activist communities in Morocco pushing for local language support nationally and Kenya's community participation in M-PESA, the mobile money ecosystem show how communities can push for or adapt to the latest innovations and best practices to force sluggish governments to catch up. Kenya has since digitized their company registration, taxation, contracting as well as other service delivery systems including bus transportation fees ticketing. The chaos in the 2019 Malawi elections marred by voter fraud and other challenges is a stark contrast to the somewhat digitized electoral process in South Africa where technology was leveraged to collect, aggregate, audit and report election results locally, provincially and nationally offering a model for transparent electoral administration for AU member states.

Urban communities must adapt and adopt smart city roadmaps inline with Agenda 2063 while rural communities can add a focus on Agriculture and cultural tourism. Integrating technology like IoT for targeted weather monitoring, resource delivery and agricultural monitoring can be a first step in creating value addition within local and regional communities. Food and agricultural processing centres can also be automated and set up to provide additional jobs to communities and thus should be demanded as part of major community investments and projects. Communities should challenge themselves to always have a brand identity, a vision and something unique or complementary to offer their neighbors and ultimately their nation or world and agriculture and tourism offer most a fighting chance for both tertiary and expert talent. Innovative water management and other green initiatives to mitigate natural disaster damage can be piloted within communities as well powered by a network of environmental and disaster preparedness support and data.

The City in The Last Digital Frontier

WHICH CITIES HOLD AFRICA'S WEALTH?
Much of Africa's wealth is concentrated in South Africa, but other high-growth cities are catching up

Throughout history, cities have stood the test of time, surviving monarchs, prophets, wars, disaster as well as outliving national borders and nationalism or tribal waves. Infact, the past and indeed the future belongs to cities both politically and economically. Cities, when managed well, become centers of

BrianAsingia.com @brianasingia #AskAsingia

connectivity, art, identity, culture and even commerce as well as all manners of freedoms. But to realize all this, these values must be embedded in tomorrow's digital platforms as part of a global ecosystem. According to the Financial Times:

> ...the academics identify two types of platform. The first, known as innovation platforms, act as the technology foundations on which other applications are built — like Microsoft's Windows, Google's Android and Amazon Web Services. The second — called transaction platforms — are marketplaces that bring together buyers and sellers, or advertisers and audiences [FT].

This city, and ideally the smart city in The Last Digital Frontier should be more than a mere branding phrase by politicians but an actualized e-city backed by e-governance tools, digital identities as well as open access data solutions for civic engagement, training, research and effective service delivery including elections.

Travel can and should also be leveraged to foster cultural exchanges, African cultural tourism and IP protection. Intra Africa travel as well as the engagement of the Global African Diaspora capable of delivering trillions in revenue as well as complementary benefits of a united and closer union with a large source of capital should be prioritized over a colonial model of "African discoverers." Africans must be allowed through their local communities to understand the value of natural resources including wildlife while also being also being supported to participate and benefit from the eco friendly and sustainable tourism efforts that put culture and environmental curation and exchanges above foreign funded conservation efforts with no local leadership and decision making. Local communities can develop tours, provide accommodation, transport and other arts and cultural efforts with proper hospitality training and technology integration for transparency and effective service delivery. The travel and tourism sector is ripe for innovation and disruption and public private partnerships at city levels can spur innovation in neighboring communities.

Cities can offer models for effective service delivery such as digitizing urban planning so maps, land titles and service centers like schools, health centers, postal offices , civic centers and other relevant locations like parks are easily accessible and utilized. The biggest challenge to service delivery is information asymmetry and knowledge gaps. Cities often offer structured management that can be leveraged to provide transparency.

Cities should lead in open data initiatives by leveraging open source and open access digital solutions. News, reports, performance data as well as other data like election data, connectivity and power as well as other critical services like weather and health alerts, transportation reliability among others. This can be extended to include offering financial inclusion and access to its residents through digital pilots as public private partnerships such as insurance plans, savings plans as well as health plans critical for the wealth and health of individuals and families within the city. New York City in the US is one example of exemplary leadership in open data initiatives and social programs though even for New York, there is always more work to be done such as improving the MTA (public transport system with better service delivery and reliability).

Cities should leverage global links and intra Africa partnerships to make AfCFTA a reality. By acting as hosts for diplomats, tourists, researchers and investors, cities and urban areas can foster a positive image of Africa that highlights our rich history, culture, natural resources and human capital talent ready for effective public private partnerships towards rapid job creation for youth and women across the continent. Mayors can define the city vision and act as ambassadors while allowing the city government to support actual project implementations for a digital innovation culture that puts culture and community values ahead of design so that they are integrated in the investment and development decisions and roadmaps. Kigali Rwanda is one city that has updated its conference infrastructure as well as cultural support to attract global and regional connects towards a dream Rwanda.

Cities should be the forts of defence against risks of automation and robotics while being hubs for reliable data, digital and physical infrastructure. Skills training centres and upgrading of public libraries to be digital innovation hubs for lectures, exhibits, research and other support materials can help communities feel included in the digital transition. Cities can also serve as hubs for IP protection and enforcement providing both legal education and policy discussions as well as counsel when needed for student and youth innovations. By extending global IP conversations to the local stage, communities can innovate aware of the challenges and responsibilities that come with creative and digital collaborations and innovations while protecting valuable services and trade secrets critical to the success of intra Africa trade and global digital commerce and logistics.

Cities are also zones for leaders in climate change and disaster preparedness to pilot, research and institutionalize strategic urban planning that integrated community needs including protection against natural disasters and risk mitigation action plans in city plans and policies. From disaster preparedness training to education around greener living and agriculture, communities can be a part of the solution to today's most pressing challenges.

Cities can also lead as centres of culture and values driven innovation and leadership. Just as language and culture evolves, so should cities to integrate this evolution into their architecture, design and strategic roadmaps. Reliable power and connectivity can help power arts and culture innovations through both digital and in person exchanges that would not only meet local needs but also be shared globally digitally. Cities must prioritize their cultural branding, identity and history to reflect the African icons, heroes and values they wish to share with the world. Communities must be enabled and supported to create and share arts and culture freely without political restrictions and intimidation. The recent troubling arts and culture policies such as restrictive film making policies in Kenya and Uganda requiring political approvals are areas of careful review so that communities and in particular arts and culture continues to thrive alongside technical and political evolution.

The Government in The Last Digital Frontier

THE SIX REGIONS OF THE AFRICAN UNION

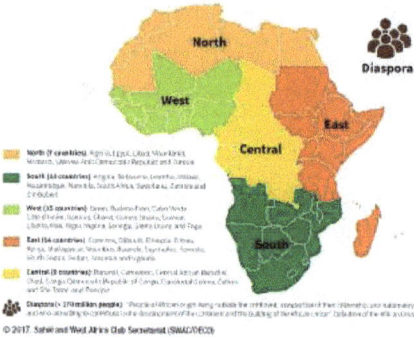

From Nationalism to Regional Governance. Note: DR Congo has applied for membership to the East African Community as of June 2019 (Source: AU.int).

That effective governance is still scarce across Africa is an understatement. Across public and private institutions, there seems to be a competition of who can get away with the most crimes or ethical violations. If colonists thought Africa barbaric they were mistaken because they have through formalized trade policies, legal protections, accounting standards and banking sophistication exported and scaled their barbaric values (CITE Barbarians at the Gate). From Frances interference in Alegria politics to CIA assassinations and foreign sabotage or regime changes, African leaders have to balance foreign puppeteering with internal strife often foreign backed through gun sales in areas like the Sudan and Congo or state capture in the case of South Africa, Cameroon among others.

This external destabilizing force present pre colonialism has been normalized since the Berlin conference and formalized through entities like the UN (no security council seat), the International Criminal Court (ICC) among others. AU and Agenda 2063 seek to reverse this trend both from a structural and mental decolonization. As has been the dismissal by the West of Asia and in particular China's rise, Africa still faces harsh criticism from the very parties that benefit from the status quo (low to no fee resource extraction and exploitation including human capital).

Governance in Africa as should be in any institution thus becomes about strategic protection against foreign influence and interference with a particular focus on non member states and ultimately a political will among leaders to put their people's agenda ahead of cheap short term bribes in exchange for generations of physical and economic captivity. This calls for Agenda 2063 to be nationalised with member states crafting their own visions that translate to their citizens. Rwanda's #VisitRwanda and #ASmallCountrywithaBIGDream are some great branding as well as visionary campaigns setting the stage from the top leadership and backed by actual effective implementation and action including healthy and clean city campaigns while a car free day in Kigali Rwanda where H.E Paul Kagame personally participated alongside his fellow Rwandans while having a leading conference infrastructure for attracting global business and experts.

With its various state institutions, democracy can not be the only way i.e the end in itself. Rather effective service delivery backed by e-governance must be prioritized over single day voting propaganda as a measure for progress. The era of extorting gratitude from citizens for protection against the imperialist (while the very leaders dine and hide wealth abroad, often preferring foreign services from health to banking and education) must be replaced with an African pride vision as shown in Rwanda, Ethiopia and Morocco as well as Libya before its foreign isolation as a contrast to Liberia's outsourcing its entire primary education system, a decision that raises more than ethical questions such as its assumption that Librarians are incapable of learning on their own or educating their own. Governance must include trust and transparency through constant civic engagement and dynamic data reports and communications on the state of the union. Rather than tax social media, governments should leverage open data services to deliver progress reports and solicit requests and feedback from the public. This real time referendum on service delivery will not only streamline budgeting but also improve taxation and fund allocations in the long term. A country worth admiring here is Taiwan and its Digital Minister as well as the youth driven gov zero initiative.

Leadership must urgently move from presidential term propaganda and rhetoric with a perpetual timeline of presidents for life to an urgent monthly and quarterly reporting mechanism at local and city levels and biannual for national and regional governments. The youth and future generations can not survive a tortoise paced planning and implementation strategy. After all, 2063 will see most of us as grandparents and the current leadership in the ancestor phase as heroes or traitors. As has been shown through metaphors and folklore, a leaking bucket or boat is bound to frustrate the owner. Africa is a leaking ship in need of urgent fixing to stop the rapid loss of wealth, access and opportunity by our generation for the sake of our children and grandchildren. Below are the critical areas governments in The Last Digital Frontier need to budget for and deliver meaningful progress on transparency and succession plans.

Agenda 2063 not only considers Africa's continental growth aspirations but acknowledges that for the whole continent to develop the premise of Agenda 2063 must be adopted at regional and country level. At the inception of Agenda 2063, the National Development Plans of Member States as well as the strategic plans of the Regional Economic Communities were reviewed and the focus areas of their development priorities have been included in the First Ten Year Implementation Plan to ensure that their priorities in the near term converge with the priority areas contained in the 50 year framework document.

The national and regional priority areas include:
Sustainable and inclusive economic growth
Human Capital Development
Agriculture/value addition and agro-businesses development

Employment generation, especially the youth and females
Social Protection
Gender / Women development and youth empowerment
Good governance including capable institutions
Infrastructural development
Science, Technology, Innovation
Manufacturing-based industrialization
Peace and Security
Culture, Arts and Sports [au.int]

National and regional priorities must be matched by reflective budget allocations and policy enforcement. Job creation, education, arts and sports are areas that must take a front seat on national budgets to offset years of neglect. Africans despite their diverse cultures have an appreciation for each other and as such cultural and sports exchanges, tournaments and commerce legislation must be funded to grow the sectors and unite the continent. Senegal and South Africa are making progress towards this front as is Nigeria through film but intra Africa collaboration and scale is lacking.

To avoid collapse of the union and other xenophobic attacks, growth and implementation must be replicable and scalable. We can not have youth always migrating to Morocco or other areas to look for opportunity. Rather, national and regional governments must be held accountable to deliver on their own commitments for their people. Political sabotage from neighbors and jealous but egocentric politicians as has been the recent cases with Uganda Rwanda border conflicts must be resolved peacefully through diplomatic and economic means.

Africans are tired of being betrayed by their leaders and are ready and willing to elect those who deliver practical and sustainable solutions to their needs in a timely and sustainable way. The youth demonstrations and recent election results across Africa demonstrate this maturity of rewarding at the polls leaders who deliver or have the political will to solve some of Africa's toughest problems as shown in South African elections where the African National Congress (ANC) lead shrunk with more power to the effective Economic Freedom Fighters (EFF) calling a spade a spade among other areas. This peaceful change in leadership that is merit driven must be emulated and supported by the AU to thrive.

While each member state has sovereignty and independence, AU member policies can be updated over time to push for more representative democracies and effective implementation of Agenda 2063. AU must make sure that conflicts like Darfur, Rwanda genocides, segregation in South Africa and child labor in the Ghanaian cocoa farms among other areas like the recent Sudan demonstrators deaths are a non-repeatable events of the past. Other areas worth resolving are the support of Morocco, Ethiopia and other North Africa states in stabilizing the Union as they have other areas of expertise including financial management and strategic investments that AU member states would benefit from in addition to increasing the AfCFTA impact for all Africans.

Beyond peaceful and transparent succession plans for leadership at all levels, governments can also leverage public private partnership success stories to institutionalize and even automate where possible, local development projects from ideation to requirements for Proposals (RFP) and capital to bid allocations. Of particular importance is also an urgent need to transition from bureaucratic report and policy generation to a crowd sourcing hybrid for ideas and insight. Similar to the US FCC (Federal Communications Commision) request for public comments and input, alot of pressing issues could be resolved if actual talented youth and experts are incentivised to contribute to and research implementation challenges in an open and transparent process. Issues like hidden 99 year lease clauses and ownership mandates could easily be spotted in more transparent and ideally digitized processes saving member states billions in revenue.

The unresolved energy crisis in most countries is one such issue where in Nigeria for example there is a lot of effort put into drafting bills and policies and minimal to no results produced on the implementation or results side let alone investing in renewable energy solutions like Solar among others. Rather than look at a problem as an opportunity to be embraced, and value created through a timely and cost effective solution, African leaders like Buhari in Nigeria and many others seem to prefer kicking the can down the road spending four years with nothing concrete to show but policy drafts not actual acts in parliament that would be enforceable. Regional monopolies in power and other critical sectors operate without accountability from term to term with no room for alternative solutions yet political propaganda pushes out communication briefs on how leaders are great for the people.

Delayed implementation has an actual cost (both economic and opportunity cost) that means AU member states cede the long future of digital revolutions to foreigners like China, the US and EU that seem to prioritize service delivery on areas of strategic and security relevance. The EU's embracing of VoIP with Skype and leveraging that to drive down roaming fees from telecoms as well as the Chinese prioritization of IP filings and recently 5G innovations race win are just a few examples of leaders betting on winning horses, understanding the long term implications of inaction for their people and status in the world. Rwanda's and Ethiopia's business, investment, energy, agriculture and transport innovations and public private partnerships to effectively deliver solutions are examples worth emulating.

For governments to also be effective, the public must also hold them accountable as should foreign donors and investors who often subsidize corrupt regimes in exchange for exclusive contracts and tax evasion. By making their voices count through votes, digital whistle blowing/shaming of corruption and community resistance to shady non transparent large private deals and projects, governance failings can be exposed, punished and ultimately minimized and replaced by effective governance powered by real time monitoring and reporting one leader, one deal and one election at a time.

The opposition in member states also need to take its responsibility more seriously to avoid propaganda opposition to ideas and policies and focus on data driven and humanity first solutions and projects. The EFF's (Economic Freedom Fighters) pressure on the ANC in South Africa is a great example of effective opposition that puts the needs of the people ahead of ego centric politics and camera time. By focusing on practical solutions to South Africa's critical challenges and embracing a pan African and non Xenophobic strategy, they have successfully led to Jacob Zuma's exit, a decrease in ANC's hold on power and an overall atmosphere of reckoning where decisions have consequences (economic, legal and political) for the ruling party. Through its actions, the EFF is not just talking but walking the talk, showing how it would govern both locally and nationally instead of behind closed doors deal making. Their values driven leadership, un faltering despite media bias, political attacks and other state capture traps and lies from other parties like the Democratic Alliance (DA); EFF left the DA-EFF coalition once they realised DA was not going to commit to agreed upon EFF values and mandates, leaves a breath of fresh air in Africa politics where a party and its leadership can actually communicate its vision, execute on it and defend the very people its fighting for against the very vices of corruption, state capture, poor service delivery, criminalization of civic engagement and activism. Their support of the fees must fall campaign and rally against activism criminalisation by the government and its state capture allies who are willing to bribe their way into institutionalizing racist policies like the school to prison pipeline common across the United States from as early as K-12/primary school.

Member state governments must also get out of the "investor friendliness" myth shared by most greedy and often corrupt advisors like PwC (South Africa) [CITE source]. The use of fear that money will leave if corruption is tackled effectively is because the counterparties are the very investors or firms benefiting from corruption and tax evasion. Until politicians, CEOs and Board member officials can lose their jobs, go to jail and have their property confiscated to return missing funds or as fines to deter future activities, governments can not claim to have people's interests at heart as stealing public funds, resources and futures is more than a crime but treason of the highest order. According to a June 13th 2019 Nairobi News article by Nahashon Musungu, the Tanzanian president is furious over port infrastructure deals with 99 year lease terms:

> "Imagine someone telling you that I will build you a port but on a condition you will not be

allowed to construct or develop any other port in the country for a specified period."

That's not all, the president added.

"That investor also demands you will also not be allowed to collect revenue (at the port they have constructed), not even TRA (Tanzania Revenue Authority) will be allowed within the premises of that investment," he explained.

"Further, you will have to guarantee them they will manage that port for 35 years. You will also have to separately settle for a lease agreement, which is different from the laws of the land for 99-years. You should also give them the mandate to transform that place as if it is their own land. While all this is happening, you need to be compensating them for the work they did to build that port. I am revealing some of these strange conditions because people have been coming here and taking advantage of Tanzania and Tanzanians. We are supposed to change."

AU member states must diligently negotiate with investors, contractors and strategic partners with an African agenda at the core. The Kenya government might have sold itself cheaply to the Chinese during negotiations to build the Standard Gauge Railway and other projects and other countries have backed out of or renegotiated Chinese infrastructure loans and deals after

Sri Lanka lost its Hambantota port to China on defaulting on the loan.

Governance, representative governance at that is more than just western versions of democracy but rather inclusive access and participation by community members such as the ancient chiefdom and current community engagement efforts by the Kingdom of Morocco. Despite challenges by past African leaders, credit must be given where it is due such as Colonel Muammar Gaddafi's successful transformation of Libya from separate camps to housing for the citizens as well as reliable water and other service delivery benefits like education until isolation from the west. It is not surprising that the west tends to isolate and put under microscope African leaders who have pro African ideas and are ready to or are succeeding at implementing them. The AfCFTA has never been more timely to alleviate this political and economic sabotage of sanctions and isolationism in a globally connected and competitive world. African leaders must learn to support each other through trade and talent exchanges for a sustained effort in attaining economic, cultural and political freedom our ancestors and leaders in our generation have died for. Isolationism and use of mercenaries should not be normalized, nor should the hypocritic use of law to criminalise constructive criticism and opposition to distract from actual effective service delivery. To do this misuse of the law would be to return to the time where apartheid, censorship and slavery among other evils was legal. Our laws and enforcement must reflect the values we hold dear and seek to fight for not those that bring shame and destruction to our very existence. There is power in numbers as well as in focusing on what already works rather than repeating past mistakes of divisive and isolationist politics and innovation.

The School in The Last Digital Frontier

Holon — Education in 2030. **Global Scenarios**
www.holoniq.com

Decolonize and Digitize Education to Compliment On Campus, Home and Field Research, Study or Innovations.

Agenda 2063 identifies several key benefits to Africans if the programmes identified in the strategic development framework are initiated and implemented in the FTYIP. Africa is expected to show improved standards of living; transformed, inclusive and sustained economies; increased levels of regional and continental integration; a population of empowered women and youth and a society in which children are cared for and protected; societies that are peaceful, demonstrate good democratic values and practice good governance principles and which preserve and enhance Africa's cultural identity [au.int].

Education and in particular "the school of life" has a critical role to play in this mandate and unfortunately for most education systems as per the recent World Bank Education report of the last 50-100 years, most of Africa's education is still caught in the colonial era of educating for specialized resource and knowledge extraction. The bureaucratic clerk system leaves many to think government is the only employer rather than venture on their own, create jobs in the community or demand more meaningful work and livable wages. Rather than teaching children and youth to fish, African schools are still serving fish, teaching imperial languages only, low wage skills and not preparing youth for the digital revolution powered by automation and global connectivity.

There are schools like the Africa Leadership Academy/University (ALU) by Fred Swanika among others are stepping up to deliver 21st century skills linked to internships and corporate collaborations. This level of dynamic, interest driven and STEAM integrated education should start at the early childhood education level, a disaster in most member states chasing political likability through free but unfunded and low staffed ineffective education programs often without even housing, food, water, let alone technology resources. One is sometimes better off relying on homeschooling and digital learning to be globally competitive due to lack of political will and incompetence in the decision making ranks of most member states.

The westward focused export of talented youth must be replaced or at least complemented with a strong Africa first education system that delivers effective programing and knowledge access both digitally and in classrooms or homes starting with early childhood education, primary and secondary as well as tertiary or higher education. In all education levels, local languages for values driven innovation, arts and culture for design and strategy, as well as science and technology including finance, leadership and communication skills and competencies must be emphasised. As the AfCFTA becomes a reality, educational and cultural exchange programs backed by arts and crafts, film, music and sports development will not only open mental and cultural borders but the long term potential for intra Africa innovation and development unlike the current siloed and often xenophobic innovation and trade policies. All these can be streamlined through digital platforms and communities that power the dynamic data driven research and analysis. Below are AU Agenda 2063 expectations that should be reflected in educational services:

Improvements in Living Standards

Real per-capita incomes would be a third more than 2013 levels.
Incidence of hunger, especially amongst Women and Youth will only be 20% of 2023 levels.
Job opportunities will be available to at least one in four people looking for work.
At least one out of every three children will be having access to kindergarten education with every child of secondary school age in school and seven out of ten of its graduates without access to tertiary education enrolled in TVET programmes.
Malnutrition, maternal, child and neo-natal

deaths as at 2013 would be reduced by half; access to anti-retroviral will be automatic and proportion of deaths attributable to HIV/AIDs and malaria would have been halved.

Nine out of ten people will have access to safe drinking water and sanitation; electricity supply and internet connectivity will be up by 50% and cities will be recycling at least 50% of the waste they generate.

Transformed, Inclusive and Sustainable Economies

GDP will be growing at 7% and at least a third of the outputs will be generated by national firms. Labour intensive manufacturing, underpinned by value addition to commodities and doubling of the total agricultural factor productivity will be attained by 2023

The beginnings of value addition blue economy – fisheries, eco-friendly coastal tourism, marine bio-technology products and port operations- will emerge.

Creative arts businesses will be contributing twice as much in real terms their 2013 contribution to GDP.

ICT penetration and contribution to real GDP in absolute terms would be double of 2013 levels.

Regional industrialization hubs linked to the global value chains and commodity exchanges will be in place by 2023.

At least 17% of terrestrial and inland water and 10% of coastal and marine areas would have been preserved and 30% of farmers, fisher folks and pastoralist will be practicing climate resilient production systems.

Integrated Africa

There will be free movement of goods, services and capital; and persons travelling to any member state could get the visa at the point of entry.
The volume of intra-African trade especially in agricultural value added products would increase threefold by 2023.
The African Customs Union, an African Common Market and an African Monetary Union will be operational by 2023.
The African Speed Train Network will have passed the inception stage and will be taking its first passengers between two connected cities.
African Skies will be open to all African Airlines.
Regional power pools boosted by at least 50% increase in power generation and the INGA dam will be operational and will contribute to the powering of the industrial transformation of the continent and comfort of the citizenry.
African Education Accreditation Agency and a common educational system are in place and the African Youth will have the choice to study at

any university and work anywhere on the continent.

Empowered Women, Youth and Children

All obstacles related to Women owing/inheriting property or business, signing a contract, owning or managing a bank account would be removed by 2023.
At least one in five women would have access to and control of productive assets.
Gender parity in control, representation, advancement will be the norm in all AU Organs and the RECs.
All forms of violence against women would have been reduced by a third in 2023.
All harmful social norms and customary practices would have ended by 2023.
The African Youth will be mobile and 15% of all new businesses will emanate from their ingenuity and talent and the proportion of 2013 youth unemployed will be reduced by at least a quarter.
Child labour exploitation, marriages, trafficking and soldiering would have ended by 2023

Well-governed, peaceful and cultural centric Africa in a Global Context

Democratic values and culture as enshrined in the African Governance Architecture would have been entrenched by 2023.

BrianAsingia.com @brianasingia #AskAsingia

At least seven out of ten people in every member state of the union will perceive elections to be free, fair and credible; democratic institutions, processes and leaders accountable; the judiciary impartial and independent; and the legislature independent and key component of the national governance process.

African Peer Review Mechanism will have been ascribed to by all Member States and its positive impact on governance metrics felt.

All guns would have been silenced by 2023.

All Member States of the Union will have in place local and national mechanisms for conflict prevention and resolution.

All Member States of the Union will have in place a dual citizen's programme for the diaspora.

The Encyclopedia Africana will be launched by the 2023 Assembly of the Union.

One in five polytechniques will be offering programmes in the creative arts and management of micro cultural enterprises to support the growth of the creative arts businesses.

Local content in all print and electronic media would have increased by 60%.

At least 30% of all cultural patrimonies would have been retrieved by 2023.

An African Space Agency would have been established by 2023.

An African Global Platform will be in place by 2017 and will contribute to an increase in the share of Africa's exports in global exports in 2023 by at least 20%.

The African Investment Bank, the African Guarantee Facility, the African Remittances Institute and at least 2 Regional Stock Exchanges would have been established and functioning. National capital markets will contribute at least 10% of development financing and the proportion of aid in the national budget will be no more than 25% of the 2013 level.

All the above targets become unachievable and ineffective if the population especially parents, children and youth are not educated, trained and offered opportunities to contribute to, own and operate/maintain the proposed solutions. Local, national and continental ownership backed by transparent digital automation and reporting is one way to guarantee minimum setbacks from trust issues, corruption and favoritism. For example youth and elders in South Africa need to be reminded of their African and carribean allies who came to their aid to put an end to the apartheid regime when the West was not moved to act for fear of disrupting their own economies that benefited from these oppressive regimes. Africans must more than anything be trained to think of each other as allies and collaborative family for the good of the continent if not for real economic freedom, for the peace and security of all. The divisive politics and foreign or corporate sabotage of communities must be replaced by human shields of love, compassion and human driven design to develop and embed human values within our solutions and innovations unlike the structural and systemic racist and often colonial values that exist in most systems including education.

Business and ultimately job creation from small to medium businesses should be supported by aggressive tax credits, incentives and funding so as to include more communities in the digital economy. By aligning education to nature and expose children and youth as well as adult learners to the AU Agenda 2063 with a call to action, spaces and opportunities for leveraging educational resources, the youth can be tapped to bring Agenda 2063 to fruition.

One way is to also collaborate with the Legal and Policy makers so that schools protect student work and innovations, balancing collaboration with commercialization and providing enforcement against IP theft by foreign academic institutions, corporations and governments as has been the case with most African research, drug tests among others such as the UK University case of Kenyan medical /biology research being registered in the UK. Deeper programs like clinical trials from foreign firms can also be better handled to increase medical and ethical compliance as well as provide better protection to communities against biomedical weapons, fake drugs and exploitation while pushing for local medical innovations to enjoy the same or better incentives and thrive. African grown herbs, natural raw materials among others such as Marijuana, health superfoods are sample projects that can be introduced to students in managed environments like school for implementation and scale within their communities. Religious hypocrisy from leaders against progressive solutions like medical Marijuana in Uganda must also come to an end, as Jesus said, man can not live on bread alone, we must accept knowledge and science at that while celebrating religious and cultural values.

While culture should always have a place and culturally relevant learning materials developed, science and facts should also be emphasized in areas where that is critical such as medicine, construction and transportation as well as digital innovation without minimizing the impact of design and culture during implementation. Practical relevance and value of medical marijuana and other traditional herbs must be protected, licenced and researched to protect African knowledge from foreign exploitation. Failure to do so is just as bad as revealing state secrets for the future is no longer just about physical might but also digital and intellectual might as shown by the recent rise of China and the subsequent panic by the US and the EU regarding the 5G innovation and other electronic trade wars [WIPO Report 2019]. Who knows what biomedical research will answer into the next century?

Education or rather the school in The Last Digital Frontier becomes one of the critical pillars necessary for survival and should thus be a priority to all stakeholders (individuals, families, leaders in both public and private life as well as strategic partners) with an urgent need to pivot from linear and often staged learning to dynamic, automated and interest driven learning backed by opportunities for job shadowing, exploration and placement as well as cross border collaboration and research. Just like libraries in Timbuktu attracted scholars from all over the world, Africa's libraries, museums, schools and institutions must thrive to offer more to their communities and by extension the world rather than looking westward for education and solutions. This is a long term mandate that must start with a real intent backed by political and individual will to decolonize education and ultimately economies, politics and culture starting with individual study, family interactions as well as civic engagement to push the agenda forward. The era of static textbooks, rarely updated to reflect practical realities is over and must evolve to introduce dynamic and immersive learning materials that make effective, affordable education and knowledge sharing accessible to all.

Inclusion and access to affordable and reliable decolonized education from early childhood is the key to breaking the cycle of poverty and colonial thinking that has kept Africa in chains while the rest of the world adapts, innovates and evolves. Freedom is not just voting on a single day but involves agency for day to day decision making including what one learns, aspires to do or be as well as the self actualization of those values and beliefs. Knowing the Africa we want is one step but the next one is to provide the tools and resources to build that Africa with minimal negative political or foreign interference. As Steve Biko would say, black consciousness is a state of mind, and the mind is always learning, adapting and evolving. Only a dynamic and adaptic school, platform and ecosystem can deliver the Africa we want should be supported moving forward.

The Last Digital Frontier by Asingia 203

The Spiritual and Religious Community in The Last Digital Frontier

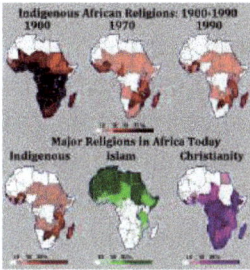

Source: Mathew White, Wikimedia.

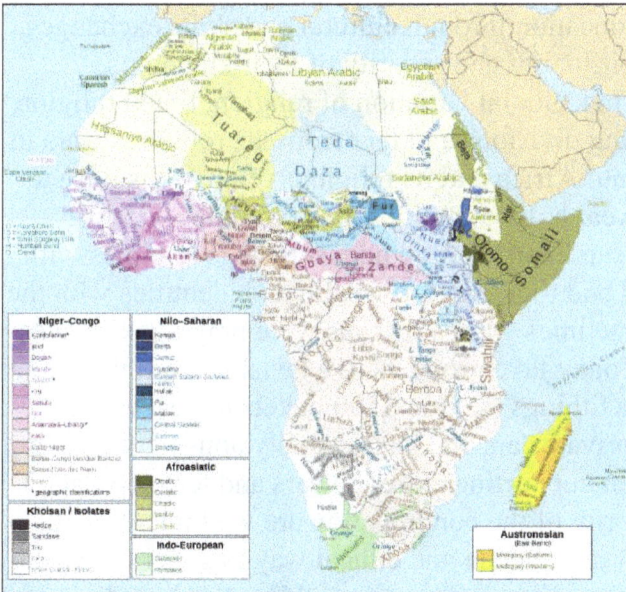

Culturally Relevant Innovations Key to Global
Competitiveness and Intra Africa Scale (Source: Wikimedia).

Spirituality, religion and faith once worked to improve communities and support the security, education and development of the people. African religions and spirituality put self love, self care and self actualisation backed by historical and ancestral roots and wisdom at the core. Islam and early christianity in areas like Egypt and Ethiopia also served the same purpose often sharing values like equity, inclusion and taking care of one another. Despite religious differences and strong political empires, Africans traded and lived amongst each other driven by bigger goals and visions around education through cultural and skills exchanges, travel, spirituality and security of their kingdoms.

The colonial variation of religion, tinted religion by bringing divisions and fear from the religious wars in Europe into Africa and its religions often as disguise to control wealth, land, politics, policy, trade and more. The African interpretation here is they gave bibles with one hand and took African wealth and identities with the other sometimes while Africans were praying with eyes closed. Today fake prophets live lavishly from their followers tithings (selling $500 tickets to heaven, owning private cars and jets, sexually abusing kids and women, or supporting extreme wars and terrorism acts). The majority of the congregation are well intentioned, seeking a moral code and ethical way to generate wealth and live their lives but are trapped in a hawky religious environment that cares less about the congregations welfare than the leaderships exemplary success at all costs. From Zimbabwe to South Africa, Mali, Egypt and Uganda among others, religious centres are turning into sources of discord rather than unity and community improvement.

While this is not reflective of all religions and centres, the global conflicts such as the sexual abuse scandals within the catholic church and the anti-christian or Jewish attacks by a few jihadists leaves the world searching for meaning within religion itself. Governments like Rwanda are taking steps to require certification and some form of theological education to reduce public abuse by "religious heads" and offer structure to religious establishments a contrast to unresolved conflicts in Nigeria, Mali and other AU member states. Agenda 2063 offers a unique opportunity for religious leaders to rally their congregations behind a pan African vision that protects religious freedoms as well as the rights and security of all Africans not as political vessels for foreign powers.

Knowledge and information asymmetry are some of the leading causes of conflict, corruption and exclusion or extraction based policies across Africa. Religious leaders can walk into a new chapter of standing for moral and ethical integrity by complimenting legal and civic engagement efforts. Religious centres, home visits and other community events can be leveraged to share and educate the public on their rights as well as the Agenda 2063 goals and expectations. By educating citizens and urging them to hold their leaders accountable, this grass roots effort can easily scale and provide the much needed understanding and coordination among the public and their leaders to get Africa into the digital era of effective service delivery and self actualization.

Unfortunately for some religions as is with some non profits, most of their existence is tied to the suffering of the people and as such some would rather communities stayed in absolute poverty and conflict rather than see their beneficiaries decrease. Here the challenge is for religious leaders to also denounce corruption upfront and put the needs of the people first (both spiritual and temporal/physical). Fair living wages, health care and education are among the few realities religious leaders can rally behind including tolerance and co-existence, a foundation for the free movement of people and services goal of Agenda 2063.

Perhaps unlike the absolute control of politics by religion and vice versa, religion and state should be separate but complementary institutions to work around fear based leadership and divisive service delivery of us vs them. Small towns like Kasese, Uganda and multireligious political leadership in Senegal (both christian and islamic presidents have been elected) are good examples of religious coexistence with about one third muslims, catholics and protestants and coexistence of other christian and African or Hindu religions in Uganda. This backed by a consistent tourism influx allows for a truly vibrant community ready for growth and development to realize Agenda 2063 for her people through contributions from all members both local and foreign.

Like cultural and non profit organizations, religious centers can also play critical roles in civic engagement, serving as election centers, health by encouraging immunization and other health campaigns as well as education and service delivery by providing information, support and accountability.

The Nonprofit/NGO in The Last Digital Frontier

One user pointed out just how common this type of photo is, writing, "A trip to Africa is not complete without the trademark poverty porn photo op." (Source: Oxygen, Twitter)

The non-profit/NGO leader and employee or volunteer suffers the same moral dilemma as the religious leader or service member. For most of Africa, nonprofits are synonymous with colonial slavery, extending imperial extraction and poverty dependency policies to continue serving as the "pretty face" of this horrid trade reality. As if that is not enough, non-profits have propagated the "dark continent" narrative, often reaping millions to billions and becoming a major employer is most areas second to government. Care, UN, Red Cross among others have their share of roles in conflicts or compromising situations. The UN for example was ineffective or to be blunt, chose in-action during the Rwandan genocide and continues to be an "observer" for serious conflicts like that of Sudan and the Congo. UN "peacekeepers" have been reported to have molested and raped young underage girls among other community atrocities in the very areas they are tasked with protecting. The Red Cross has had its share of spending about

80% of donor funds on salaries and operations and not actual service delivery or aid to intended recipients. This is almost true for most nonprofits and NGOs who prefer fancy hotels, restaurants, cars, inflated purchases among others to become the dream job for most women and youth trapped by poverty and corrupt officials. The above failings of nonprofits and NGOs do not reflect the genuine effort and sacrifice by dedicated volunteers globally who often risk their lives to save others, feed and educate millions across Africa and the world. Their service and effort is commended but the advocacy here is for a strategic transition for "poverty porn" to actual social and economic transformation that leaves individuals, families and communities in much better states than the current poverty dependency and refugee camps not resettlement initiatives.

For the UN to fully reflect its commitment to global peace and representation, a UN security council seat must be offered to African member states rotating as per the AU mandate. Otherwise, Africa will continue to be at the losing end of imperial sabotage, assassinations, coups as well as privatized military and propaganda conflicts as is the case of Apartheid in South Africa, Genocide in Rwanda and Sudan as well as assassinations in areas like Libya among others. Other non-profits should also align with Agenda 2063 and deliver metrics that reflect both quantitative and qualitative changes in communities they serve. Tax deductible status should not be politicized or be used as ways to hide money, avoid taxes as well as clean up dirty money, rather the tax deductions should be put to work in delivering civic engagement, education, healthcare, skills training, housing and investment support among other Agenda 2063 priorities to compliment the government and private sector efforts.

The public private partnerships and coordinations as well as transparent RFP guidelines and processes are a necessary part of this transformation. Digital dashboards and automated reports similar to those used by election centres and market data can help provide the necessary visualization and transparency for all stakeholders including the public and donors. The conflict between public and private service delivery can not reach extreme levels to the point where communities themselves are left unserviced with no one held accountable. For example in Port Elizabeth, South Africa - The Department of Water and Sanitation will be paying private contractors R10 million for humanitarian work already carried out by Gift of the Givers in water scarce Makhanda in the Eastern Cape.

> "We successfully drilled 15 boreholes, tested the water, which is a huge cost, brought in special filtration systems designed by us, delivered bottled water, water by truck and did everything possible to assist the community as that was the priority. In all this time we had not received a single cent from any government institution. The costs were rising daily. Thus far the intervention has cost us R15 million."

> Sooliman said the department started engaging with the organisation and, without exaggeration, more than 50 hours of meetings have been held over 13 weeks.

> "But the best came from DSW on Freedom Day, when President Cyril Ramaphosa, was addressing the

nation. They told us to move our trucks as there is no water crisis in Makhanda. Ironically, the president mentioned in his speech that there can be no freedom if there is no water in Makhanda."

"This week we received the most incredible feedback from DWS. They said only companies from Grahamstown can be paid for the drought intervention so accordingly, a private consultancy will be paid R1.2 million for work related to boreholes (we did the consultancy work, drew up a plan to save the city and sited the boreholes), another company will be paid R7 million for boreholes (which we drilled) and a third company will be paid R1.9 million for electrical work to connect boreholes which we drilled at Waainek (and which we have not been compensated for) to the treatment plant," said Sooliman. [IOL SA News]

The above is an example of politics and egos driving service delivery. The politicians and private companies, like the police in most western films, arrive after the fact, a little too late. Adequate planning, RFP guidelines and budget allocations can help develop a culture of transparent but consistent service delivery and improvements with clear visibility of stakeholders and accountable parties for both service delivery and payments. Beneficiaries too should have a voice in the short term delivery as well as the community cost and expectations for long term maintenance and use of service delivery infrastructure across generations. Service delivery must transition from crisis intervention to pre-planning and long term strategic investments and incentives separate from short term political games and needs.

Nonprofits and NGOs can not be replacements for basic government service delivery but rather should be amplifiers or proponents of public private initiatives and efforts offering a buffer to political scavengers and capitalist monopolies. Effective service delivery should be designed and implemented with local skills training and job creation at the core for long term sustainability and scalability of both public and private service delivery and impact. Foundations and non profit donations should not be excuses or replacements for moral and ethical obligations of both politicians and private companies as they serve the public. Humanity must have a place in politics and innovation or private enterprise and nonprofits/NGOs can help drive that conversation with a push for direct transformation with government and private enterprise.

The state capture inquiries in South Africa into Zuma, "White Monopoly Capital" as per EFF, "Rhodes must fall" campaign despite the well intentioned Rhodes Scholars program and other Nelson Mandela initiatives show the folly of using non-profits to clean blood money or hide corrupt initiatives by public and private enterprises. Transparency and genuine service delivery must be the high road of the land not just cash donations and token charity regardless of source and cost of said propaganda. As youth are trained in civic engagement, public policy, law and international affairs, let us not blindly elevate organizations and politicians that grow and benefit at the expense of the public and citizens of AU member states. Agenda 2063 can and should be the guiding compass for our generation when in doubt. Donor and Board transparency is achievable especially if recipient communities have visibility and direct participation into these processes and programs through dynamic digital visualizations, reports, fund transfers, local employment and representative decision making not just consultation.

The Private Enterprise in The Last Digital Frontier

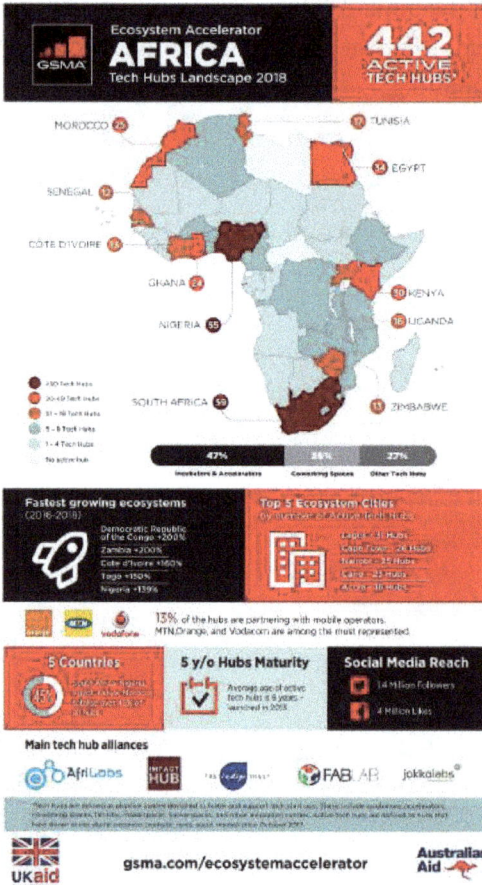

Several continental frameworks have been developed to address the development of key sectors such as Agriculture, trade, transport, energy and mining. These sectors are seen as key in enabling Member States of the Union to achieve their development goals. To ensure coherence and convergence, these frameworks have been captured in the priority areas of the First Ten Year Implementation Plan. The continental frameworks include the Comprehensive African Agricultural Development Programme (CAADP), The Programme for Infrastructural Development in Africa (PIDA), The African Mining Vision (AMV), Science Technology Innovation Strategy for Africa (STISA), Boosting Intra African Trade (BIAT), and Accelerated Industrial Development for Africa (AIDA) [au.it].

As SME's are the backbone of Africa's economies, albeit in the shadow of tax evading, extraction focused and unlivable wage multinationals and conglomerates, the private sector should aspire to create meaningful employment, social economic development and education through inclusive savings, investments and credit policies. Here too, The Last Digital Frontier IoTs (Identity, Ownership, Trust and Scale) are just as important. The continental frameworks thus become bridges and roadmaps for private public partnerships that can scale and support intra Africa trade in the long term while creating meaningful employment from the short term. Family businesses, family offices for capital and even homeschooling all have roles to play in Agenda 2063. In reality, empowered families and homes especially the middle class provide the social economic stability fundamental to sustainable growth and economic inclusion.

CAADP is a continental initiative to help African countries eliminate hunger and reduce poverty by raising economic growth through agriculture-led development. Through CAADP, African governments agreed to allocate at least 10% of national budgets to agriculture and rural development, and to achieve agricultural growth rates of at least 6% per annum. Underlying these main targets are targets for reducing poverty and malnutrition, for increasing productivity and farm incomes, and for improvements in the sustainability of agricultural production and use of natural resources. CAADP also supports member states to enhance resilience to climate variability through development of disaster preparedness policies and strategies and early warning response systems and social safety nets [au.it]. CAADP has 4 priority areas namely:

Extending the area under sustainable land management and reliable water control systems

Improving rural infrastructure and trade-related capacities for market access

Increasing food supply, reducing hunger, and improving responses to food emergency crises

Improving agriculture research, technology dissemination and adoption

In addition CAADP places emphasis on African ownership and African leadership to set the agricultural agenda and the stage for agricultural change. This change emphasises Africans truly being the drivers of CAADP, rather than the more typical case of leadership and direction coming from donors or other international partners. CAADP is thus an inward looking policy framework where African leaders who have championed CAADP in their countries can influence their counterparts towards agricultural transformation.

The Programme for Infrastructure Development in Africa, (PIDA), provides a common framework for African stakeholders to build the infrastructure necessary for more integrated transport, energy, ICT and trans-boundary water networks to boost trade, spark growth and create jobs. As a multi sector programme PIDA) is dedicated to facilitating continental integration through improved regional infrastructure and implementing it will help address the infrastructure deficit that severely hampers Africa's competitiveness in the world market, transform the way business is done and help deliver a well-connected and prosperous Africa. PIDA's long-term strategic planning for Africa's regional infrastructure has been conducted under the coordination of the African Union Commission, the African Union NEPAD Planning and Coordinating Agency, the United Nations Economic Commission for Africa and the African Development Bank in cooperation with all African stakeholders.

The African Mining Vision (AMV) calls for the "Transparent, equitable and optimal exploitation of mineral resources to underpin broad-based sustainable growth and socio-economic development." The AMV envisages an African mining sector that is:

Knowledge-driven and contributes to growth & development which is fully integrated into a single African market;

Sustainable and well-governed and effectively garners and deploys resource rents, is safe, healthy, gender & ethnically inclusive, environmentally friendly, socially responsible and appreciated by surrounding communities;

A key component of a diversified, vibrant and globally competitive industrialising African economy;

Helping to establish a competitive African infrastructure platform, through the maximisation of its propulsive local & regional economic linkages;

Optimising Africa's finite mineral resource endowments and that is diversified, incorporating both high value metals and lower value industrial minerals at both commercial and small-scale levels;

Harnessing the potential of artisanal and small-scale mining to stimulate local/national entrepreneurship, improve livelihoods and advance integrated rural social and economic development;

A major player in a vibrant and competitive national, continental and international capital and commodity markets.

The AU Science, Technology and Innovation Strategy for Africa (STISA) places science, technology and innovation at the epicentre of Africa's socio-economic development and growth and the impact the sciences can have across critical sectors such as agriculture, energy, environment, health,

infrastructure development, mining, security and water among others. The strategy envisions an Africa whose transformation is led by innovation and which will create a Knowledge-based Economy. STISA is anchored on six (6) priority areas namely:
Eradication of Hunger and Achieving Food Security
Prevention and Control of Diseases
Communication (Physical and Intellectual Mobility)
Protection of our Space
Living together in peace & harmony to build the society
Wealth Creation.
The strategy further defines four mutually reinforcing pillars which are prerequisite conditions for its success namely: building and/or upgrading research infrastructures; enhancing professional and technical competencies; promoting entrepreneurship and innovation; and providing an enabling environment for Science Technology and Innovation (STI) development in the African continent.

SUMMARY OF STISA-2024 PRIORITY AREAS

Research and/or innovation areas

1 Eradicate Hunger and ensure Food and Nutrition Security
Agriculture/Agronomy in terms of cultivation technique, seeds, soil and climate
Industrial chain in terms of conservation and/or transformation and distribution
infrastructure and techniques

2 Prevent and Control Diseases and ensure
Well-being
Better understanding of endemic diseases -
HIV/AIDS, Malaria Hemoglobinopathie
Maternal and Child Health
Traditional Medicine
3 Communication (Physical & Intellectual Mobility)
Physical communication in terms of land, air, river
and maritime routes equipment
and infrastructure and energy
Promoting local materials
Intellectual communications in terms of ICT
4 Protect our Space
Environmental Protection including climate change
studies
Biodiversity and Atmospheric Physics
Space technologies, maritime and sub-maritime
exploration
Knowledge of the water cycle and river systems as
well as river basin management
5 Live Together – Build the Society
Citizenship, History and Shared values
Pan Africanism and Regional integration
Governance and Democracy, City Management,
Mobility
Urban Hydrology and Hydraulics
Urban waste management
6 Create Wealth
Education and Human Resource Development
Exploitation and management of mineral resources,
forests, aquatics, marines etc.

Management of water resources
Find out more about STISA and our other
programmes aimed to boost innovation and to grow
science and technology on the continent

The objective of BIAT to deepen Africa's
market integration and significantly increasing the
volume of trade that African countries undertake
amongst themselves from the current levels of about
10-13% to 25% or more within the next decade. The
BIAT Action Plan provides for the assessment of
Africa's overall trade flows and the potential for
boosting intra-African trade by addressing key
priority areas (both supply-side and demand-side) and
identifying which areas are important to make trade
an important driver of regional integration, structural
transformation and development in Africa. The BIAT
Action Plan identifies seven (7) critical pillars
(Clusters) to address challenges facing intra-African
trade such as infrastructural bottlenecks, improving
trade facilitation, enhancing opportunities for
intra-African trade through trade information
networks, addressing financial needs of traders and
economic operators through improved finance,
addressing adjustment costs associated with FTAs
and trade liberalisation to ensure equitable outcomes
for Member States. Specifically, the Clusters are:
Trade Policy
Trade Facilitation
Productive Capacity
Trade Related Infrastructure

Trade Finance

Trade Information and Factor Market integration

Find out more about our initiatives to foster regional integration and to boost intra-African trade

The Action Plan for the Accelerated Industrial Development of Africa (AIDA), is a pan-African programme developed by the United Nations Industrial Development Organization (UNIDO) in 2008 at the request of the African Union, together with African governments and the private sector. The strategy aims to mobilise both financial and nonfinancial resources and enhance Africa's industrial performance. The AIDA focuses on driving the integration of industrialisation in national development policies especially in poverty alleviation strategies, development and implementation of an industrial policy with priority accorded to maximizing the use of local productive capacities and inputs, through value addition and local processing of the abundant natural resources of the country. AIDA also seeks to support the development of small-scale and rural industries, including the informal sectors as well as intermediate and capital goods industries with high linkages to other sectors of the economy as potential sources of employment creation. The AIDA strategy further seeks to improve Investment and Mining Codes to support local processing of mineral resources whilst at the same time encouraging mineral resources- rich countries to set aside portions of commodity price-surge related premiums for investment in programmes/projects of economic diversification. The programme also expects the continent to leverage Africa's Partnerships, especially with the Newly Industrializing and Emerging Powers of the South, for the development and transfer of technology, for the establishment of joint industrial enterprises in Africa, and for greater market access for African manufactured products.

Private enterprise is and should be the bedrock of Africapitalism. However, like China and most of Asia, a mixed economy approach should initially be embraced to have smoother transitions and not the World Bank restructuring rhetoric effects of Jamaica and South Africa among other areas that brought in dumping of cheaper goods and services at the expense of local industry as well as stiff default penalties. The multilateral approach to trade and negotiation thus allows various partners to compete or bid for the best offer delivering a favourable outcome than bilateral engagements. China and Russia's success at managing and scaling state funded or owned institutions should be a model for service delivery improvements that compliment the private sector but also grow economies.

With a particular emphasis on digital innovations and economies, local innovators should be backed by state capital to help gain the necessary growth capital needed for scale. Exit plans through joint ventures, Mergers and Acquisitions (M&A) and listings on public markets ideally a single pan African stock and futures exchange would provide ways for states to recoup their capital and distribute the wealth to the public and other institutions. Political backing is already an unfair but necessary factor for success on the continent either directly or indirectly and hence governments can provide critical investments through public private partnerships to scale infrastructure needs in energy, connectivity, transport and policy enforcement as well as capital formation for projects that are beneficial to all via public private partnerships.

Almost every sector across Africa is open to innovation and disruption should monopoly licences be revoked or opened to more players in areas like resource mining, mineral and raw materials processing, packaging and logistics, health care, insurance, education among others. At a minimum, there is money to be made from digitization of African economies including government service delivery through bids for contracts and Request for Proposals (RFPs) as well as the subsequent monitoring and evaluation processes.

Because of historical abuses and extraction policies by large multinationals, government should streamline joint venture and M&A policies for local firms to partner, franchise or merge for both scale and value addition. In other words, SMEs and family owned businesses can grow and scale through a network effect, bundling under a larger brand either as equal local, regional, continental or even global partners. The relevant terms of agreement can vary depending on state and private entity priorities but the need for strategic collaborations and mergers to achieve the necessary scale for both cost, operational and cross border trade savings is inevitable. Consolidation thus becomes a necessary evil that must be tracked and perhaps lightly regulated as long as there are competitive environments to foster other participants.

Through the single African passport, single air transport as well as the AfCFTA that among other things provides for dual citizenship options for Africans in the global diaspora, Africans around the world can easily join existing ventures or start new ones and coordinate global empires within a short time due to the improved legal, policy and capital institutions and frameworks. With the right strategic advisors and consultants, there is a lot of value add and wealth creation that can be generated from global empires formed this way with physical and digital networks around the world. China and other major digital players have leveraged this ecosystem that taps the Diaspora when the time for global expansion arises and Africa must not only emulate but improve the value addition.

With digitized company registration, incorporation and board management, operations and intra Africa trade compliance, private enterprises as seen in Kenya, Rwanda and Ethiopia can compliment government efforts to bring about effective and scalable social economic transformations. Private companies must also take an active role in talent development both in creative, digital and financial skills training as well as setting up and supporting employee savings and investment options. Africans must grow to understand financial instruments from an early age to make deal making and value creation a faster trust based process. Otherwise family politics and cultural biases that are often emotionally charged replace good business acumen.

The Foreign Government in The Last Digital Frontier

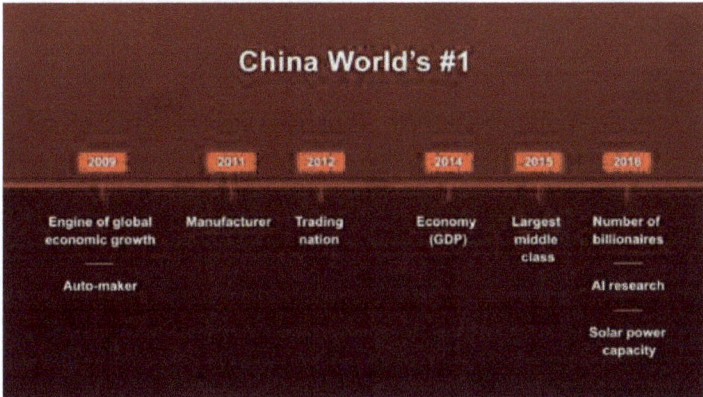

Global Geopolitics is Changing. Is Africa Ready? (Source: TED Talk, Understanding the Rise of China by Martin Jacques)

China's Belt and Road Initiative
130 countries are participating at some level as of April 2019

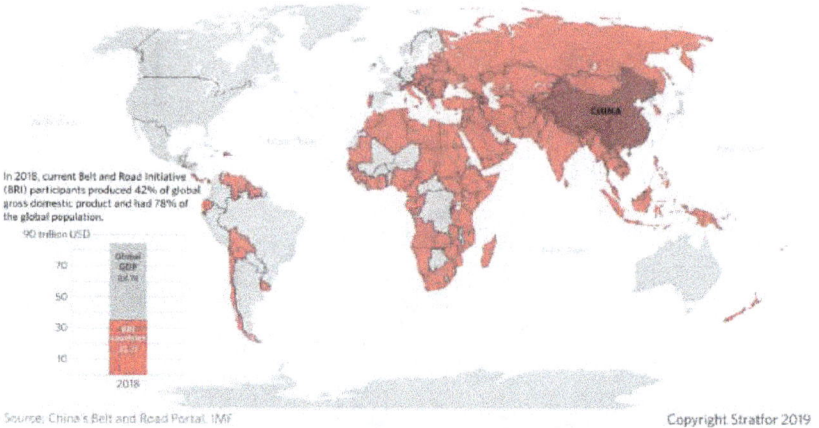

In 2018, current Belt and Road Initiative (BRI) participants produced 42% of global gross domestic product and had 78% of the global population.

Source: China's Belt and Road Portal, IMF

Copyright Stratfor 2019

Africa needs its youth and experts for smart negotiations.

Yuval Noah Harari an Israeli Scientist, Historian and author notes that Nuclear war, Climate change, and Technological disruption are humanities main challenges e.g genetic human experiments of which the solution is Trust and a global safety net against A.I's autonomation and bioengineering in innovation centers and minimal impact in low cost manufacturing and processing. He further adds that Nationalism is not about hating foreigners but taking care of your compatriots without abandoning old national loyalists or opening borders to unlimited immigrants advocating globalism i.e a commitment to some common rules regulating the relation between nations such as the World Cup. He however falls short by advocating for the EU to serve as a model for the world as they have successfully balanced "Harmony without Uniformity" [Harari, Author Homedues].

Perhaps the EU model may have worked for Europe but the EU relations with the world prove otherwise that it is not one to be replicated explicitly as are their internal tensions on extremism, racial politics among other challenges like Brexit. China's silk road initiative, BRICS among other options like AU's AfCFTA are models to watch as they all offer options and not bilateral agreements but rather a multilateral approach to negotiation [Parag Khanna, Author The Future is Asian].

The flagship projects of Agenda 2063 refers to key programmes and initiatives which have been identified as key to accelerating Africa's economic growth and development as well as promoting our common identity by celebrating our history and our vibrant culture.The Flagship projects encompass amongst others infrastructure, education, science, technology, arts and culture as well as initiatives to secure peace on the continent [au.int]. These are areas that should serve as a vote of confidence for foreign governments in terms of the trade, investments and collaboration opportunities within The Last Digital Frontier. Education and talent exchanges, cybersecurity and innovation collaborations as well as ultimately a seat on the UN security council are various opportunities for meaningful collaborations that uplift the people of Africa while benefiting the world. Below are AU projects in the works:

1. INTEGRATED HIGH SPEED TRAIN NETWORK

The project aims to connect all African capitals and commercial centres through an African High Speed Train Network thereby facilitating the movement of goods, factor services and people. The increased connectivity by rail also aims to reduce transport costs and relieve congestion of current and future systems. Rail complementing road, air and sea transit is a priority part of the Transport, Infrastructure and Energy Initiatives [au.int].

Important to note is that this project must be backed by a reliable power and connectivity initiative and could as well serve as the pilot for wifi on trains or free wifi in centres where trains make stops to foster local innovation and digitization. Digital identity, ticketing and logistics support as well as cyber security can only be possible with reliable power and connectivity. This increase in mobility will not only support and grow existing businesses but lead to whole new ventures that both serve and compliment the transport and logistics sector.

Ethiopia is one country making headway in renewing rail transport across Africa to serve her people. Despite cost, maintenance and other logistics challenges, trains in cities like New York and D.C in the United States of America make commutes possible for millions who would otherwise struggle to get around. Investing in inclusive and sustainable transport systems like rail, air , water (ferry) and road (buses) among others with complimentary wifi and renewable energy power sources like solar would not only make a strong foundation for smart cities but also connect Africans not just across borders but also digitally as well as through trade and travel.

Urban planning and in particular smart city initiatives must be coordinated and included in the implementation so that the net impact of the infrastructure is smart, scalable and future proof both from an operations and maintenance perspective. Scheduling, routes, employment and funding sources must be such that they increase inclusion and access and not the opposite as has been the case of some subsidized transport initiatives in Southern Africa that end up benefiting well to do communities who use certain modes of transport like rail and bus more than others in smaller towns. The ultimate network must work in coordination with other air, water, land and or automated transport alternatives. An example here is making sure strategic initiatives like China's belt and road initiative augment Agenda 2063 projects for an accelerated and people first economic development backed by local job creation, retention and growth.

2. FORMULATION OF AN AFRICAN COMMODITIES STRATEGY

The development of a continental commodities strategy is seen as key to enabling African countries to add value, extract higher rents from their commodities, integrate into the Global Value chains, and promote vertical and horizontal diversification anchored in value addition and local content development. The strategy aims to transform Africa from simply being a raw materials supplier for the rest of the world to a continent that actively uses its own resources to ensure the economic development of Africans through programmes to boost Africa's production and trade in commodities [au.int].

Countries like South Africa, Ghana, Nigeria, Congo, Angola among others that are mostly mineral and commodities export dependent are member states that should lead the transition to people first sustainable resource processing and value addition in contrast to the current colonial extraction and export focused process that relies on low wage labor to near slave labor as well as tax evasion to work. Even Agricultural produce like Cocoa in Ghana, coffee in Uganda, peanuts in Tanzania suffer the same value losses. Communities are tricked into accepting exploitative monopolies with the governments blessings leaving generations of wealth inequality as shown by the recent decision by Ghana and Ivory Coast farmers to halt cocoa sales without adequate compensation in June 2019 [Fortune].

The AU goal to mandate local mining and commodities firms to coordinate with local mineral or food processing options prior to export increases value both from job creation as well as export value from the refined products and services. The energy, technology and electronics spaces could benefit from this transformational shift moving from import only electronics import to local assembly and ultimately component manufacturing and specialization. Resources critical to infrastructure, transport, communications and security should be improved and infact local futures markets developed as well to allow for Africans to participate, own and benefit from natural resource processing and agriculture. This is another area that needs tax incentives and other strategic investments to allow the commitment and long term investments of both human and financial capital so as to achieve meaningful impact on both local, intra Africa and global levels once the transition to people first value addition and processing is complete.

An ecosystem development approach has to be undertaken with various phases or stages modeled for both public, private and communities to engage with and execute. For example, schools have a role to play in training talent for these opportunities as do city planners and community leaders on how they can manage and add value to resources before they leave communities. Nationalism and pan Africanism should be culturally embedded in these campaigns to create a legitimate sense of ownership that is backed by transparent digital systems for planning, budgeting and trading as well as investing in these sectors. This can start from something as simple as real time valuation of resources marked to both local and global market demand and providing the legal support for labor and wage protections so that meaningful employment with a living wage as a minimum becomes a reality.

3. ESTABLISHMENT OF THE AFRICAN CONTINENTAL FREE TRADE AREA (AfCFTA)

Accelerate intra-African trade and boost Africa's trading position in the global marketplace. The AfCFTA aims to significantly accelerate growth of intra-Africa trade and use trade more effectively as an engine of growth and sustainable development by doubling intra-Africa trade, strengthening Africa's common voice and policy space in global trade negotiations. [au.int]

Ownership in initiatives to foster regional integration and to boost intra-African trade can be realized through education, civic engagement, tax incentives and public private partnerships. Africa's less than 20% intra Africa trade is way lower than the 30-50% global average in Asia, EU and other regions. Moreover, within regional communities like the East

African Community or ECOWAS (Economic Community of West African States) is actually higher and closer to 100% in East Africa when it comes to free movement of people. These regional initiatives can be highlighted and leveraged to bring intra Africa Trade into fruition [au.int].

Critics argue that the failed history of regional integration often politicized (first through colonial efforts and later by some like Libya's Muammar Gaddafi who funded the Union when he was isolated by the US and Europe etc) but they miss the point of who stands to benefit from a single agenda or voice Africa and who stands to lose or perhaps not loot the continent. Indeed while the vision is challenging in itself, the realization may not be if there is no political will. Like Asia, we already have cultural collaborations across demographics and thus the goal is not uniformity but mutual respect and co-existence.

With different countries and regions having different resources, strategic locations and opportunities, there is no need for African countries to compete on every front amongst each other. Sector based collaborations such as in Mining, Agriculture, Industrialization, Automation, IP Enforcement, Taxation and Investments or Savings can all be implemented through digital systems that enable for transparency and real time collaboration to the benefit of the masses not tax evading corporations. Non technical factors like deferred tax incentives or exemptions for innovative SMEs in critical areas complimented with lower fees and taxes as well as legal protection would not only make doing business in Africa attractive but also lower operational costs and the relevant capital needs that are often inaccessible.

4. THE AFRICAN PASSPORT AND FREE MOVEMENT OF PEOPLE

Remove restrictions on Africans ability to travel, work and live within their own continent. The initiative aims at transforming Africa's laws, which remain generally restrictive on movement of people despite political commitments to bring down borders with a view to promoting the issuance of visas by Member States to enhance the free movement of all African citizens in all African countries. This is one of the many initiatives to remove border restrictions and foster continental integration by promoting free movement of Africans within the continent [au.int].

Digitizing this single passport and backing it with biometric data is also critical to reducing fraud and easing access and service delivery. Travel delays, lines and lost document fees as well as renewal or replacement costs can be lowered or eliminated for the millions who are left out of the travel and cross border trade sectors due to the length and bureaucracy around documents and permit processing. The benefits are also complementary to other identity based services like employment, banking, insurance, credit and taxation.

India, China, the EU and in particular areas like Estonia can be learnt from in implementing global service delivery backed by digital identities. Companies like Akoin.io, by Akon are leveraging and innovating on digital identities backed by blockchain for credit and other token based services that could power the intra Africa and global trade of the future. Companies like Automation Anywhere combine innovation with training as well as free accessible solutions and it is the same approach of inclusion and access that should be approached by the AU commission and the AU member states in practically implementing Agenda 2063.

The single African Passport must not only be powerful in Africa but also globally. Foreign governments must be lobbied and educated on the value for immigration both for diplomacy and cultural exchange as well as education and trade. The old colonial world of preferences given to former colonies at the expense of other economies must be replaced with a single African voice and mandate for transparency and mutual respect in both global trade and security.

5. SILENCING THE GUNS BY 2020

To achieve the goals of Agenda 2063, Africa needs to work towards ending all wars, civil conflicts, gender-based violence, violent conflicts and preventing genocide. In addition, progress in the areas are to be monitored through the establishment and operationalisation of an African Human Security Index (AHSI) [au.int].

Peacekeeping activities through AU Commision organs, job creation and transparency through fighting corruption, localizing economic impact and youth engagement are all pieces of the puzzle. To speak of peace one must acknowledge the role of security in all its forms (physical, spiritual/religious, social, economic and health among others). For most member states, democracy begins and ends with elections rather than continuing to thrive through transparency, accountability and civic engagement of citizens.

The recent allocation of 25% of the AU commission budget towards the Peace Fund is a strong indication of the priority of this issue. However, soft measures like exemplary leadership, accountability and people first negotiations can help eliminate or avoid some of today's conflicts often going back generations. From land to food and water security, peace cannot exist in nations without vision and an inclusive service delivery roadmap for her people. Government thus becomes the first lever of accountability after individuals/families being responsible for their home and travel experiences. Neighbors as member states can also support peaceful conflict resolutions through regional bodies and AU agencies. Most importantly, the AU should avoid the isolationist or bullying tactics of the west that reward only political or trade allies at the cost of human lives within different nation states with different points of view. Haiti, Cuba, Iran, Zimbabwe,Libya and now Sudan are some of the states whose population has suffered more due to western isolationist policies that put politics over humanity.

Africa has the tools and resources to achieve the above goal but needs the political will that aggressively implement Agenda 2063 with African youth and women needs at the forefront. By committing to a people or humanity first service delivery, politicians who win should be those that delivery effectively. Likewise, peer to peer negotiations would include local community support and engagement. For long standing conflicts such as Ethiopia and Eritrea conflict, the open outreach and sincere desire for a people first solution can be replicated across the continent rather than allowing individuals to hold Agenda 2063 hostage who may often be backed by foreign or private interests against the community or citizens. The state capture in South Africa, corporate militia sponsored women rapes in the Congo and civil war in Cameroon are examples of conflicts driven by greed and not a genuine desire for equal economic freedom and engagement by citizens.

6. IMPLEMENTATION OF THE GRAND INGA DAM PROJECT

The development of the Inga Dam is expected to generate 43,200 MW of power, to support current regional power pools and their combined service to transform Africa from traditional to modern sources of energy and ensure access of all Africans to clean and affordable electricity [au.int].

Transport, Infrastructure and Energy Initiatives are timely but not enough attention is being paid to renewable energies and their actualization especially solar power where most of Africa would be a beneficiary with new innovative solar storage solutions. Without reliable power, Africa will continue to be "a dark continent" as the high power fees for often unreliable power and connectivity leave African SMEs at a global disadvantage to innovators in smart cities with free Wifi and affordable and reliable power.

Africans needs to look beyond traditional power sources and regional monopolies and embrace scalable offgrid solutions as a transitional step towards effective, affordable and reliable energy infrastructure grids. The government dependent power projects as seen in South Africa, Uganda, Nigeria among many AU member states are merely a photo-opportunity but a disgrace to the talent and youth of the motherland. No one deserves monopoly status or complete government support with taxpayer funds who still have to pay for unreliable power if that entity can not deliver quality service that powers the economic engines of member states (SMEs).

Sectors like mineral resource mining and oil drilling that are power dependent could leverage off grid sustainable solutions and offload excess energy to the grid for local communities to benefit. Friendly policies from tax incentives to soft loans among others should be extended to innovations and investments in renewable energy like solar as well as offgrid energy generation and storage solutions. A five to ten year write off is needed to aggressively address the energy desserts across Africa.

7. ESTABLISHMENT OF A SINGLE AFRICAN AIR-TRANSPORT MARKET (SAATM)

The SAATM aims to ensure intra-regional connectivity between the capital cities of Africa and create a single unified air transport market in Africa, as an impetus to the continent's economic integration and growth agenda. SAATM provides for the full liberalisation of intra-African air transport services in terms of market access, traffic rights for scheduled and freight air services by eligible airlines thereby improving air services connectivity and air carrier efficiencies. It removes restrictions on ownership and provides for the full liberalisation of frequencies, tariffs and capacity. It also provides eligibility criteria for African community carriers, safety and security standards, mechanisms for fair competition and dispute settlement as well as consumer protection [au.int].

Beyond the benefits of trade, tourism growth and intra Africa air transport innovations, there is also room for emergency and disaster management solutions, security and privacy innovations as well as the critical connectivity challenges. Indeed Rwandair and Ethiopian Airlines have led the way in streamlining the transit routes, collaborating and innovating to serve Africans and the world with Africa owned and operated airlines and innovative solutions. For Africa to secure her place at the global trade table, AU member states must take basic foundational pillars seriously such as secure and operating airports, clear modernized policies on air transport innovations like drones that make the air space accessible to most Africans and most importantly a push for cities to participate and boost local flights.

Thus, as seen with the challenges of foreign reliance on talent and expertise as well as technology such as the recent unregulated use of the Boeing 737 Max and subsequent crash by the aircraft used by Ethiopian airlines leaving loss of lives for many across Africa and the world. The US laissez faire approach to innovation that often has little consumer protection can not and should not be imported as is. Africa, through the AU bodies and the commision must enact air transport and innovation policies that put the lives and safety of Africans first and foremost. Caution must be taken to also avoid the European extreme conservatism that may not be great for some innovations but rather a Humanity first African approach should be developed, as a hybrid of best practices that deliver innovation in fields like automated flights and drones while bringing humanity to AI innovations and robotics.

Such implementation is only possible if identity, ownership, trust and scalability are integrated in both policy design and implementation leaving AU member states to not only monitor the growth and development of air transport industry but also make sure that cross border taxation, visa and other intra Africa collaboration challenges are reduced and minimized for the effective mobility of goods, services as well as human capital. Technology through flight monitoring, scheduling and security has a role to place in modernising and unifying Africa's single air transport market.

8. ESTABLISHMENT OF AN ANNUAL AFRICAN ECONOMIC FORUM

The annual African Economic Forum, is a multi-stakeholder meeting that brings together the African political leadership, the private sector, academia and civil society to reflect on how to accelerate Africa's economic transformation harnessing its vast resources to enhance the development of the African people. The forum discusses key opportunities as well as the constraints that hamper economic development and proposes measures to be taken to realise the Aspirations and goals of Agenda 2063 [au.int].

The economic Forum alongside the investment forum are becoming not just education, policy formation but also invest and fundraising vehicles bringing together billions in commitment towards intra Africa initiatives from power to connectivity and trade. Of critical relevance is the need for women and youth to be included and represented as equal stakeholders at these events and conferences. The challenge for Africa is no longer a lack of talent or solutions but rather the ability and indeed political will of leaders to implement the right solutions for their people as opposed to the foreign backed and multinational first mandate that excludes people and indeed citizens both present and future from deliberations.

It is exciting that the global stage The World Economic Forum (WEF) 2020 will actually be in Addis Ababa, Ethiopia as a testament to the new relevance of Africa as The Last Digital Frontier. America developed by allowing cities at one time to compete around branding and infrastructure of malls, parks and convention centers. Cities like Chicago, New York "The Big Apple" among others rebranded themselves to offer space for civic engagement, job creation and models for urban innovations in architecture and social engineering. African cities need to leverage this opportunity to push for rotating host roles so that both intra Africa and global conferences and summits look to Africa for hosting, angeging and tracking progress of such efforts as has been the case for Kigali, Rwanda.

There is no reason for young African talent to always pay thousands of dollars and Euros to fly westward only to discuss or perhaps listen to western experts offer their African expertise. Africa must embrace its role as a new global panelist and moderator, host great and timely conversations on the challenges of our time while leading in presentation options and practical solutions that put humanity not corporate elitism first. Public private engagement in social economic development is needed but we must never forget that technology, policy and any human innovation should seek to make like better for humanity and not the opposite.

9. ESTABLISHMENT OF THE AFRICAN FINANCIAL INSTITUTIONS

The creation of African Continental Financial Institutions aims at accelerating integration and socio-economic development of the continent through the establishment of organisations which will play a pivotal role in the mobilization of resources and management of the African financial sector. The financial institutions envisaged to promote economic integration are the African Investment Bank and Pan African Stock Exchange; the African Monetary Fund and the African Central Bank [au.int].

Of all the above, equal and impactful, the Pan African Stock Exchange would create the most impact through financial inclusion and access if policies are drafted and enforced to support individual and family participation in stocks, futures and other derivative asset ownership. While structural and public investments create a foundation for long term growth and innovation, stock exchanges and financial markets create opportunities for deploying savings as investments, increasing individual or fund ownership of private companies or ventures within an economy and reap the rewards of any upsides.

Financial literacy and education at all levels from early childhood education to primary, secondary and tertiary or higher education should be supported for Africans to understand their options and opportunities as well as develop a savings and investment culture. Financial markets and assets while familiar to the rich and powerful are hardly in the vocabulary of the communities excluded from participating but with the ability to provide liquidity and volume at scale and in aggregate such as via savings plans, group investments among other networks.

Local capital mobilization backed by dynamic ownership and soon digital assets or other trust based systems would compliment other AU financial institutions and transfer decision making from an elite few to the participation and support of the member states citizenry. The other benefits here are that African companies list locally first instead of always looking westward for growth capital. African innovations backed by African capital and sustained by intra Africa trade with a global Diaspora or global market compliments are the fruits of successful pan African financial institutions.

10. THE PAN-AFRICAN E-NETWORK

This aims to put in place policies and strategies that will lead to transformative e-applications and services in Africa; especially the intra-African broad band terrestrial infrastructure; and cyber security, making the information revolution the basis for service delivery in the bio and nanotechnology industries and ultimately transform Africa into an e-Society [au.int].

While this is ambitious and well intentioned, the core challenges of lack of reliable power and connectivity infrastructure must be in place to coordinate the next stages.

Broadband infrastructure, fiber optic cables alongside power lines, 5G networks for connectivity as well as innovative VoiP (voice over internet) solutions bundled with IoT devices can deliver the e-network needed for secure, scalable and dynamic service delivery.

As seen with the recent Google refusal to update its Android operating system in Huawei products as a result of US China trade wars (a decision later delayed or reversed when the US reversed the restriction) Huawei, a chinese based mobile manufacturer reliant on US mobile chips is nonetheless ready with its own operating system. The danger here is that of vendor lock in where there is a lack of ownership to critical infrastructure and IP, often a result of lack of sound policy like IP enforcement,innovative talent and capital to fund and scale innovations.

Africa's e-Society can not thrive in captivity of foreign powers and agencies and as such policies, talent and capital must be availed for Africa focused and owned innovations as e-Society and the relevant cybersecurity challenges including trade wars impact the real independence and sustainability of economies at scale. Open source and licensed innovations are great as long as strong mutual agreements that are enforceable protect users and economies that benefit. The lack of interoperability, backwards compatibility and even forward integration of siloed systems can create challenges so an API driven, microservices architecture and service driven innovation culture must be developed and sustained as part of a critical cybersecurity and indeed economic and physical security of AU member states.

11. AFRICA OUTER SPACE STRATEGY

The Africa outer space strategy aims to strengthen Africa's use of outer space to bolster its development. Outer space is of critical importance to the development of Africa in all fields: agriculture, disaster management, remote sensing, climate forecast, banking and finance, as well as defence and security. Africa's access to space technology products is no longer a matter of luxury and there is a need to speed up access to these technologies and products. New developments in satellite technologies make these accessible to African countries and appropriate policies and strategies are required to develop a regional market for space products in Africa [au.int].

Digital IDs with the right security clearance can enhance global collaboration around knowledge sharing, research, innovation and pilots for scale. African youth need to be supported in exchange programs, digital learning and coordination of intra Africa launch centers. The unique opportunities are leveraging space innovations to improve Africa's connectivity and energy challenges before transitioning to travel, disaster management among other areas. Connectivity backed by reliable power delivers the digital infrastructure needed to create, own, secure and scale space focused innovations.

For the innovative youth as well as the global community, this is an open front for meaningful public private partnerships and collaborations. The recent Hurricane Idai in Southern Africa, floods, earthquakes and other disasters can be better tracked, analyzed and managed with great space innovations. More importantly, communities can be inspired and engaged in these innovations so that they are not only aware of their individual roles and contributions but also aspire to and contribute to a safer and sustainable future.

Transparency from weather data, space tests or flight schedules as well as security defense systems would not only develop a prepared, engaged and responsible citizenry but also provide jobs and research opportunities for the youth as well as the international collaboration with other space agencies. With regional launchpads and sites ideally close to the coast, on islands or remote desert areas, space innovation and exploration can be a boost to tourism, innovation and cybersecurity complimenting Agenda 2063 across various fronts like peace and security, improved Agriculture and air travel.

12. AN AFRICAN VIRTUAL AND E-UNIVERSITY

This project aims to use ICT based programmes to increase access to tertiary and continuing education in Africa by reaching large numbers of students and professionals in multiple sites simultaneously. It aims to develop relevant and high quality Open, Distance and eLearning (ODeL) resources to offer students guaranteed access to the University from anywhere in the world and anytime (24 hours a day, 7 days a week [au.int].

Digital learning (elearning) is a timely solution to Africa's urgent need to train and prepare youth for the 21st century and beyond. STEAM based programs that combine science, technology, engineering, arts and mathematics can all be delivered digitally via apps and platforms with schools and global research centers as strategic partners. Employers can integrate learning goals into their work culture for supervised talent development in both digital skills and social intelligence. These can all be powered by digital IDs that allow for seamless intra Africa talent deployment and human capital development.

Digital certificates can thus be linked to the digital IDs allowing African youth and women including people with disabilities and adult learners to benefit from mobile and screen based learning that can be both interactive and immersive with the help of VR/AR and 360 video experiences. Automated learning experiences can and would integrate career guidance and global knowledge sets to compliment local languages, culture and innovations.

The elearning architecture allows for greater trust within the job market allowing for robust skills development that is accessible and scalable. Peer to peer research and other digital verification systems and processes can help locate, verify and reward the best talent with relevant job, leadership and innovation opportunities across borders and cultures. These digital and creative skills certificates can be extended to be globally transferable for multinationals that need Africa based talent delivering knowledgeable and skilled youth driven economies.

The eLearning platform becomes a digital bridge across Africa's borders and barriers for millions of African youth seeking inclusion and access to the leadership, trade and innovation opportunities across Africa and the world. Success here can be tracked by the 21st century skills developed ideally to complimented Agenda 2063 as well as by the youth jobs created.

13. CYBER SECURITY

The decision to adopt Cyber Security as a flagship programme of Agenda 2063 is a clear indication that Africa needs to not only incorporate in its development plans the rapid changes brought about by emerging technologies, but also to ensure that these technologies are used for the benefit of African individuals, institutions or nation states by ensuring data protection and safety online. The Cyber Security project is guided by the African Union Convention on Cyber Security and Personal Data Protection [au.int].

Cyber Security is critical to the digital identities strategy. With proposed single passport and dual citizenship for Africans and the global diaspora, the digital identities powered by complimentary electronic and biometric data will allow Africans and the Diaspora to engage with government, public and the private sectors. These identities then power safe travel, ownership of assets and wealth creation and distribution.

Ownership powered by digital identities creates new risks and opportunities and a strong cybersecurity framework, automated threat detection and resolution procedures are critical. As STEAM curriculum are implemented, employee and civil servant training on best cybersecurity practices as well as digital privacy and security best practices should be integrated. The human errors can be minimized by beefing up due diligence at the issuance of passports with associated digital and biometric records. A transparent and bribe free way is the best way to guarantee inclusion and access at scale for the masses.

Trust based relationships power digital commerce and service delivery and Africa has been painted by the western media as a trustless society. The corruption narrative often supported by our leaders does not help much. However, the new technologies like blockchain, A.I and open source software and architectures can bring transparency and accessibility to a process driven by secrecy and favor swapping. The garbage in/garbage out data philosophy still holds where corrupt or incorrect digital IDs and data are entered in Africa's cybersecurity systems without ample data cleaning and single source of truth resolution. There is a need and room for a comprehensive digital ID initiative like that implemented in China or India with targeted service delivery and enhanced security.

Scale can thus be achieved by creating global African IDs, African vs Diaspora IDs, regional IDs as well as national and city/local IDs for government and private sector engagement, service delivery as well as scale across borders and cultures. These digital IDs or peronas of a single ID can thus be extended by third party apps and services to provide a secure and connected populace ready for civic engagement, education, innovation, research, trade and leadership.

14. GREAT AFRICAN MUSEUM

The African Charter for African Cultural Renaissance recognises the important role that culture plays in mobilising and unifying people around common ideals and promoting

African culture to build the ideals of Pan-Africanism. The Great African Museum project aims to create awareness about Africa's vast, dynamic and diverse cultural artefacts and the influence Africa has had and continues to have on the various cultures of the world in areas such as art, music, language, science, and so on. The Great African Museum will be a focal centre for preserving and promoting the African cultural heritage [au.int].

As has been echoed by various African leaders calling for the return of looted art by colonial empires and global museums, and actualized in part by the Black Culture Museum in Senegal as an example of what is possible,foreign governments have a role to play in accelerating this dream. The return of African art, regalia and ornaments by countries like Britain, France, Belgium among others would allow Africa to be the owner and custodian of its history and narratives. This not only has decolonizing history benefits but allows future generations to build on this legacy in art, culture, science and leadership innovations.

There is the obvious benefit from global tourism, a multibillion dollar industry from the global diaspora to foreigners who want to relive this rich and diverse culture on the motherland. The billions of tourism revenue lost each year due to African art being scattered all over the world where Africans have to leave their continent to appreciate their art and history is not only a disgrace but also lack of prioritization on the part of the African leadership in collaboration with the global leaders. Culture and art can be the foundation for global trust and collaboration as has been shown through sports like the Olympics and World Cup among others. Art and Culture should be and is the foundation on which global cooperation flourishes and only those countries that honor this code, by returning looted and illegally obtained art whether as part of colonial efforts or wars would receive mutual trade and knowledge exchange terms in contrast to those who do not.

Tertiary sectors bound to benefit from the Great African Museum are tourism, film, arts and culture, fashion, education and social cultural status and leadership/diplomacy. Africa can champion the next general of multicultural innovation based on centuries and millennia of history and culture that can be traced to the origins of humankind. By owning our culture and reshaping the narratives, Africa's vision, dreams and goals can be better vocalized, expressed and defended at the global stage, delivering a faster path towards the Africa we want. Digitizing the art and creating new and immersive digital experiences for education, travel and research purposes would allow scalable access to Africa's rich history by all Africans, the global diaspora and the world.

Decolonizing Geography and Geopolitics.

Bibliography and Research

APPENDIX A - All African Union Websites

DEPARTMENT WEBSITES
Chairperson of the AU - https://au.int/web/en/cpau
Chairperson of the AUC - http://cpauc.au.int
Deputy Chairperson of the AUC - http://dcpauc.au.int
Economic Affairs - http://ea.au.int
HRST - http://hrst.au.int
Infrastructure and Energy - http://ie.au.int
Legal - http://legal.au.int
Political Affairs - http://pa.au.int
Peace and Security - http://peaceau.org
Rural Economy & Agriculture - http://rea.au.int
Social Affairs - http://sa.au.int
Trade and Industry - http://ti.au.int
Women, Gender - http://wgd.au.int
Department of Citizens and Diaspora Organizations (CIDO) -
http://pages.au.int/cido

PROJECT WEBSITES

MEAS - Multilateral Environmental Agreements -
http://meas.au.int

AUCC - AU Climate Chage - http://aucc.au.int
AUHerald - http://auherald.au.int
PATTEC - http://pattec.au.int
AMESD - http://amesd.au.int
AMERT - http://amert.au.int
AGENDA2063 - http://agenda2063.au.int

SUMMITS

22nd AU Summit - http://summits.au.int/en/22ndsummit
21st AU Summit - http://summits.au.int/en/21stsummit
20th AU Summit - http://summits.au.int/en/20thsummit
18th AU Summit - http://summits.au.int/en/18thsummit
17th AU Summit - http://summits.au.int/en/17thsummit
16th AU Summit - http://summits.au.int/en/16thsummit
ICC - Extraordinary Summit - http://summits.au.int/en/icc
Diaspora Summit 2012 -
http://summits.au.int/en/diasporasummit2012

SPECIAL WEBSITES
Home of CAADP Events - http://pages.au.int/caadpyoa
AU Commission on International Law (AUCIL) -
http://pages.au.int/aucil
ANTICOR- Advisory Board on Corruption -
http://www.auanticorruption.org/auac/en
International Public Sector Accounting Standards (IPSAS) -
http://pages.au.int/ipsas
19th Conference of Parties - COP19/CMP9 -
http://pages.au.int/cop19
AXIS - African Internet Exchange System -

http://pages.au.int/axis

Afro-Arab Partnership - http://pages.au.int/afroarab

End Hunger - http://pages.au.int/endhunger

Cairo Office - http://pages.au.int/cairo

Comprehensive Africa Agriculture Development Programme |
CAADP - http://pages.au.int/caadp

ECOSOCC - http://pages.au.int/ECOSOCC

Information Society Division - http://pages.au.int/infosoc

The African Group of Negotiators - http://pages.au.int/agn

Rio+20 - http://pages.au.int/rio20

ACERWC | The African Committee of Experts on the Rights
and Welfare of the Child - http://pages.au.int/acerwc

Informal Economy - http://pages.au.int/informaleconomy

COP17 - http://pages.au.int/cop17

Africa Food and Nutrition Security Day -
http://pages.au.int/afnsd

2nd Congress of African Economists -
http://pages.au.int/economists

One Africa - One Voice Against Hunger -
http://pages.au.int/savinglives

2050 Africa's Integrated Maritime Strategy -
http://pages.au.int/maritime

Institut Africain pour les Versements (AIR) -
http://pages.au.int/versements

African Institute for Remittances (AIR) Project -
http://pages.au.int/remittance

CARMMA: Campaign on Accelerated Reduction of Maternal,
New Born and Child Mortality - http://pages.au.int/carmma

AUC Library - https://au.int/en/auclibrary

E-recruitment: AU Careers website -

http://pages.au.int/e-recruitment
African Shared Values - http://www.africansharedvalues.org

APPENDIX B - Bibliography

Emeagwali, Gloria T. "History of Science in

Non-Western Traditions: Africa." History of

Science Society. History of Science Society,

2018.

https://hssonline.org/resources/teaching/teaching

_nonwestern/teaching_nonwestern_africa/.

"African Elections by Africanarguments · MapHub."

MapHub. African Arguments, 2019.

https://maphub.net/africanarguments/african-elec

tions.

Akinosho, Toyin. "Nigeria: How Buhari Failed to Solve

Nigeria's Energy Crisis in His First Term."

allAfrica.com. Premium Times, May 26, 2019.

https://allafrica.com/stories/201905260026.html.

Al Jazeera. "Sudan Military Calls for Joint AU, Ethiopia

Transition Plan." Breaking News, World News

and Video from Al Jazeera. Al Jazeera, June 23,

2019.

https://www.aljazeera.com/amp/news/2019/06/su

dan-military-calls-joint-au-ethiopia-transition-pla

n-190623223306227.html.

"Artificial Intelligence for Contracts." Evisort. Accessed

June 22, 2019. https://evisort.com/.

Asemota, Victor. "Makers and Innovation." The

Guardian Nigeria News - Nigeria and World

News, June 19, 2019.

https://m.guardian.ng/technology/makers-and-inn

ovation/.

Asemota, Victor. "Makers and Innovation." The

Guardian Nigeria News - Nigeria and World

News. Guardian NG, June 19, 2019.

https://guardian.ng/technology/makers-and-innov

ation/.

Asingia, Brian. "Brain Asingia - The Last Digital

Frontier: Africa Focused Innovations with Global

Scale and Impact." Google Slides. Google, 2019.

https://docs.google.com/presentation/d/1a1IdgQ2

ahTTcXvMkGF_tbwE6qAH1xW2Ax0xvuKYm

peI/edit?usp=drivesdk.

Brobeck, Edvin. "Visualization the Global Digital

Divide." Mapiful, November 22, 2017.

https://www.mapiful.com/visualization-global-di

gital-divide/.

Byanyima, Winnie, and Oxfam International. "We Have
Built an Unequal World. Here's How We Can
Change It." World Economic Forum, 2019.
https://www.weforum.org/agenda/2018/01/we-ha
ve-built-an-unequal-world-heres-how-we-can-ch
ange-it.

"Congolese Storyteller Is Breathing New Life into
African Mythologies." Design Indaba. Design
Indaba. Accessed June 22, 2019.
https://www.designindaba.com/articles/creative-
work/congolese-storyteller-breathing-new-life-afr
ican-mythologies.

David. "What to Know About Prince Mohammed Bin
Zayed, the Arab Ruler Swaying Trump." The
New York Times. The New York Times, June 2,

2019.

https://www.nytimes.com/2019/06/02/world/mid
dleeast/prince-mohammed-bin-zayed.html.

Dignan, Larry. "IBM Launches Watson Tools for
Agriculture." ZDNet. ZDNet, May 22, 2019.
https://www.zdnet.com/article/ibm-launches-wat
son-tools-for-agriculture/.

Dignan, Larry. "IBM Launches Watson Tools for
Agriculture." ZDNet. ZDNet, May 22, 2019.
https://www.zdnet.com/article/ibm-launches-wat
son-tools-for-agriculture/.

"Education." World Bank. Accessed June 24, 2019.
https://www.worldbank.org/en/topic/education.

"EFF Manifesto Launch 2019: Five Main Talking
Points." The South African, February 2, 2019.

https://www.thesouthafrican.com/news/eff-manif
esto-launch-2019-talking-points/.

Elsevier. "Africa Generates Less than 1% of the World's
Research; Data Analytics Can Change That."
Elsevier Connect. Accessed June 24, 2019.
https://www.elsevier.com/connect/africa-generate
s-less-than-1-of-the-worlds-research-data-analyti
cs-can-change-that.

Genzlinger, Neil. "Henry Louis Gates Jr.'s 'Africa's
Great Civilizations,' Shows a Continent's Grand
Sweep." The New York Times. The New York
Times, February 28, 2017.
https://www.nytimes.com/2017/02/28/arts/pbs-af
ricas-great-civilizations-review-henry-louis-gates
.html.

"History of Science and Technology in Africa."

Wikipedia. Wikimedia Foundation, May 5, 2019.

https://en.wikipedia.org/wiki/History_of_science

_and_technology_in_Africa.

"HolonIQ. Global Education Market Intelligence."

HolonIQ. Accessed June 24, 2019.

https://www.holoniq.com/.

"Home - Africa Information Highway Portal." Knoema.

Accessed June 24, 2019.

http://dataportal.opendataforafrica.org/.

"Interesting Facts about the Great Walls of Benin in

Nigeria, One of the World's Largest Man-Made

Earth Structures." Face2Face Africa, July 4,

2018.

https://face2faceafrica.com/article/interesting-fac

ts-about-the-great-walls-of-benin-in-nigeria-one-

of-the-worlds-largest-man-made-earth-structures.

Kazungu, Kalume. "Kenya: Agency - Lamu Port a

Threat to Existence of Historical Sites."

allAfrica.com. Daily Nation KE, May 16, 2019.

https://allafrica.com/stories/201905160241.html.

"Magufuli Reveals 'Strange' Conditions Set by Investors

for African Countries – VIDEO." Nairobi News,

June 13, 2019.

http://nairobinews.nation.co.ke/news/magufuli-ex

poses-strange-conditions-set-by-investors-for-afri

can-countries.

Maifadi, Kamogelo. "General Data Protection

Regulation (GDPR) in Africa: So What?"

Lexology, May 22, 2019.

https://www.lexology.com/library/detail.aspx?g=
f9d05505-ae8c-473e-a322-40c376fd8217.

"Microsoft's Blockchain Obsession, Including ID Push,
Is Good for Bitcoin." CCN Markets, May 15,
2019.
https://www.ccn.com/microsoft-blockchain-id-go
od-bitcoin.

"National Geographic Magazine." National Geographic
Magazine. Accessed June 24, 2019.
http://ngm.nationalgeographic.com/big-idea/02/q
ueens-genes.

News, Al Jazeera. "Global Foreign Direct Investment Is
down, but Not in Africa." Breaking News, World
News and Video from Al Jazeera. Al Jazeera,
June 13, 2019.

https://www.aljazeera.com/amp/ajimpact/global-f
oreign-direct-investment-africa-19061220181884
3.html.

Noonan, Laura. "China Leads Blockchain Patent
Applications." Financial Times. Financial Times,
March 25, 2018.
https://www.ft.com/content/197db4c8-2e92-11e8
-9b4b-bc4b9f08f381.

Nordling, Linda. "Africa's Science Academy Leads Push
for Ethical Data Use." Nature News. Nature
Publishing Group, June 18, 2019.
https://www.nature.com/articles/d41586-019-018
94-0.

Olowosejeje, Samuel Ayokunle. "Nigeria's Unreliable
Electricity Costs Its Economy $29 Bln a

Year-Solar Power Would Save Billions." Quartz

Africa. Quartz, June 3, 2019.

https://qz.com/africa/1632978/nigeria-solar-powe

r-could-fix-costly-electricity-problems/.

Paul, Kari. "San Francisco Is First US City to Ban Police

Use of Facial Recognition Tech." The Guardian.

Guardian News and Media, May 15, 2019.

https://www.theguardian.com/us-news/2019/may

/14/san-francisco-facial-recognition-police-ban.

Paul, Kari. "San Francisco Is First US City to Ban Police

Use of Facial Recognition Tech." The Guardian.

Guardian News and Media, May 15, 2019.

https://www.theguardian.com/us-news/2019/may

/14/san-francisco-facial-recognition-police-ban.

Pilling, David. "Complaints That Jumia Is Not African

  Ring Hollow." Financial Times. Financial Times,

  May 8, 2019.

    https://www.ft.com/content/95e28f88-719a-11e9

    -bf5c-6eeb837566c5.

"RaceAhead: A New Nielsen Report Puts Black Buying

  Power at $1.2 Trillion." Fortune, 2019.

    http://fortune.com/2018/02/28/raceahead-nielsen-

    report-black-buying-power/?utm_campaign=soci

    al-button-sharing&utm_medium=social&utm_so

    urce=twitt.

Sain, Raahil. "Government to Pay R10m to Private

  Contractors for Work Gift of the Givers Was

  Already Doing." IOL News, May 16, 2019.

    https://www.iol.co.za/news/south-africa/eastern-c

ape/government-to-pay-r10m-to-private-contract

ors-for-work-gift-of-the-givers-was-already-doin

g-23320512.

Sain, Raahil. "Government to Pay R10m to Private

Contractors for Work Gift of the Givers Was

Already Doing." IOL News. IOL News SA, May

16, 2019.

https://www.iol.co.za/news/south-africa/eastern-c

ape/government-to-pay-r10m-to-private-contract

ors-for-work-gift-of-the-givers-was-already-doin

g-23320512.

Sanger, David E. "Trump Wants to Wall Off Huawei,

but the Digital World Bridles at Barriers." The

New York Times. The New York Times, May

27, 2019.

https://www.nytimes.com/2019/05/27/us/politics/
us-huawei-berlin-wall.html.

Saurine, Angela. "Travel - Did the Dutch 'Steal' This
African Food?" BBC. BBC, May 9, 2019.
http://www.bbc.com/travel/story/20190508-did-t
he-dutch-steal-this-african-food.

Schreuer, Milan. "Belgium Apologizes for Kidnapping
Children From African Colonies." The New
York Times. The New York Times, April 4,
2019.
https://www.nytimes.com/2019/04/04/world/euro
pe/belgium-kidnapping-congo-rwanda-burundi.ht
ml.

"SPECIAL REPORTS." IOA. IOA News SA, 2019.
https://www.inonafrica.com/special-reports/.

Staff, Digital Phablet. "Huawei's New OS Hongmeng Is
60 Times Faster Than Android." Digital Phablet,
2019.
https://www.digitalphablet.com/huawei-new-os-h
ongmeng-60-times-faster-than-android/.

"Statistics." African Development Bank. Accessed June
24, 2019.
https://www.afdb.org/en/knowledge/statistics/.

Tech, Aptan. "Microsoft Development Centres to Boast
Tech Skills, Develop Tailored Solutions for
Africa." aptantech. Aptan Tech, May 15, 2019.
https://aptantech.com/2019/05/microsoft-develop
ment-centres-to-boast-tech-skills-develop-tailore
d-solutions-for-africa/.

"The African Regional Intellectual Property

Organization (ARIPO)." The African Regional

Intellectual Property Organization ARIPO.

Accessed June 24, 2019. http://www.aripo.org/.

"The Next Africa | Jake Bright | Macmillan." US

Macmillan. Accessed June 24, 2019.

https://us.macmillan.com/books/9781250063717.

Tugend, Alina. "How A.I. Can Help Handle Severe

Weather." The New York Times. The New York

Times, May 12, 2019.

https://www.nytimes.com/2019/05/12/climate/art

ificial-intelligence-climate-change.html.

"Uganda: Germany Withholds Aid Money From

Uganda." allAfrica.com. DW, May 25, 2019.

https://allafrica.com/stories/201905250058.html.

Union, African. "Reporting on Africa Visa Openness."

Visa Openness Index. African Union, 2019.

https://www.visaopenness.org/.

Waters, Richard. "Uber Offers Chastening Lesson for

Platform Businesses of the Future." Financial

Times. Financial Times, May 16, 2019.

https://www.ft.com/content/4a632d62-77f1-11e9

-be7d-6d846537acab.

"Welcome to SITA." SITA. Accessed June 24, 2019.

http://www.sita.co.za/.

"WIPO Technology Trends 2019 – Artificial

Intelligence." WIPO. World Intellectual Property

Office, 2019.

https://www.wipo.int/publications/en/details.jsp?i

d=4386.

Zachary, G. Pascal. "As Qaddafi Died, So Did His

Craziest Dream and Mistake: Pan-Africanism."

The Atlantic. Atlantic Media Company, October

24, 2011.

https://www.theatlantic.com/international/archive

/2011/10/as-qaddafi-died-so-did-his-craziest-drea

m-and-mistake-pan-africanism/247247/.

"Export Impact For Good." ITC. Accessed June 10,

2019.

http://www.intracen.org/itc/market-info-tools/stati

stics-export-product-country-monthly/.

"The Great Human Migration." Smithsonian.com. July

01, 2008. Accessed June 20, 2019.

https://www.smithsonianmag.com/history/the-grea

t-human-migration-13561/.

"The Responsibility of Brand and Trademarks Owners in
an Increasingly Health Conscious World: A
Balancing Exercise or a Threat to Intellectual
Property?" The African Regional Intellectual
Property Organization ARIPO. Accessed June 10,
2019.
https://www.aripo.org/success-stories/the-responsi
bility-of-brand-and-trademarks-owners-in-an-incre
asingly-health-conscious-world-a-balancing-exerci
se-or-a-threat-to-intellectual-property/.

China/Northeast Asia Collection. Washington, D.C.:
Institute for National Strategic Studies, National
Defense University, 2006.

Acharya, Amitav. *Asia Rising: Who Is Leading?*
Singapore: World Scientific, 2008.

AfDB Data Portal. Accessed June 10, 2019.

https://projectsportal.afdb.org/dataportal/.

Bunker, Stephen G., and Paul S. Ciccantell. *East Asia and the Global Economy: Japan's Ascent, with Implications for China's Future*. Baltimore: Johns Hopkins University Press, 2007.

Dana, Leo Paul. *Entrepreneurship in Pacific Asia: Past, Present & Future*. Singapore: World Scientific, 1999.

Höflich, Peter. *Asia's Banking CEOs: The Future of Finance in Asia*. Singapore: John Wiley & Sons (Asia), 2008.

Khanna, Parag. *The Future Is Asian: Commerce, Conflict, and Culture in the 21st Century*. New York: Simon & Schuster, 2019.

McAuliffe, Marie, Adrian Kitimbo, Migration Policy

Research Division, International Organization for

Migration, Gordon Institute of Business Science,

and University of Pretoria. "African Migration:

What the Numbers Really Tell Us." World

Economic Forum. Accessed June 10, 2019.

https://www.weforum.org/agenda/2018/06/heres-t

he-truth-about-african-migration/.

S, Balaji. "Equity Market - Africa Information Highway

Portal." Knoema. November 27, 2016. Accessed

June 10, 2019.

http://dataportal.opendataforafrica.org/sgapcqe/eq

uity-market.

Senarclens, Pierre De. *International Conflict Research:*

Paradigms, Geopolitics, Rationality, Enemy

Images, Arms Control, Ethnic Dimensions.

Oxford: Basil Blackwell for Unesco, 1991.

Starr, John Bryan. *The Future of US-China Relations.*

New York: New York University Press, 1981.

Stiglitz, Joseph E., and Shahid Yusuf. *Rethinking the*

East Asia Miracle. Washington, D.C.: World

Bank, 2001.

WIPO Publish. Accessed June 10, 2019.

http://regionalip.aripo.org/wopublish-search/publi

c/designs?2.

The Last Digital Frontier by Asingia 281

The Last Digital Frontier

This book tells a long overdue and timeless story of the rise of mankind in Africa, uncovers inventions and innovations across the continent throughout time, and paints a forecast of its digital revolution in the 21st century and beyond. The book provides a compelling historic and forward-looking exploration of "the last digital frontier" of access and inclusion, Africa, and its potential to lead, host, and create the innovation breakthroughs of the future. Pre-order now: www.brianasingia.com

"Technology is a tool for progress towards a better society." - ASINGIA, @brianasingia

ASINGIA, CEO DreamGalaxy Platform and DreamAfrica Consulting, has over 10 years involvement in the intersection of economy, business development, environment, technology and the arts, with a focus on Africa. He began his career at Wall Street's The New York Stock Exchange where he started as a Business Analyst in Enterprise Architecture's CORE Technology group and left as an Associate in the Product Management group. Through his work with startups and consulting, he has engaged governments, diplomats, educational institutions, and programs like Creative Lab Paris, Traction Camp by the World Bank, TED Residency by TED, and Entrepreneurs for Impact MBA by ALTIS, Milan (Tangaza University Business Model Winner 2016). He has spoken at or attended trainings and conferences such as African Billionaire Tony Elumelu Entrepreneur Network (TEF), Africa Trade and Investment Summit (ATIGS), Concordia, Ivy Business Schools, and alma mater networks including: Lafayette College, International House NYC (as a Shelby Davis Scholar) and the United World College (UWC) alumni community.

ASINGIA believes Africans must seize this moment to capture and document the truth of their past, so as to learn and grow from it. He co-publishes the Last Digital Frontier Report, Podcast and writes books and scripts for film and tv. Join him at

www.brianasingia.com @brianasingia #AskAsingia

www.ingramcontent.com/pod-product-compliance
Lightning Source LLC
Chambersburg PA
CBHW051849090426
42811CB00034B/2274/J